Principles of Ethics

ANTONIO ROSMINI

PRINCIPLES OF ETHICS

Translated by
TERENCE WATSON
and
DENIS CLEARY

FOWLER WRIGHT BOOKS
LEOMINSTER

© 1988 D. Cleary and T. Watson
Rosmini House, Woodbine Road
Durham DH1 5DR, UK.

ISBN 0 85244 148 7

Translated from
Principi della Scienza Morale
Intra, 1867

Cover photo: Milford Track, New Zealand

Typeset by Litho Link Limited, Welshpool, UK.
Printed by The Camelot Press, Southampton, UK.

Note

Square brackets [ ] indicate an omission or an editor's note or addition.

Omitted footnotes are indicated by °.

References to other works of Rosmini are given by paragraph number unless otherwise stated.

Paragraph numbers in this book are the work of the translators.

Scripture quotations are from the RSV (Common Bible) unless otherwise stated.

Preface
to the
Works of Moral Philosophy

1. I want to offer in this preface an ordered description of the nature of moral sciences, of the sphere within which they are to be found, and of their natural division. First, the nature of moral sciences.

Because human beings are cognitive and active, human life is concerned with *theory* and *practice*.[1] The same cannot be said, strictly speaking, about philosophy which is never *action* but always *consideration*, whatever the subject under consideration. Philosophy is entirely and essentially *theoretical*. Nevertheless, because it deals with action or practice we have become accustomed to speaking about *practical philosophy* instead of *the theory of practice*.

This kind of linguistic shorthand, however, is dangerous. It would be far better — and it is extremely important, generally speaking — to use a longer, more exact phrase, which safeguards the genuine meaning of words, than to lay ourselves open to error by preferring misleading brevity to clarity.

We shall not follow the usual practice therefore of separating theoretical from practical philosophy, but consider philosophy as two theories, one concerned with how beings *exist* and act, and the other with ourselves and the way in which we *have to act*.

2. These two great divisons of philosophical teaching are not *formally* distinguished. Their difference does not lie in their mode of being because both are meditative; they differ only in the objects they contemplate. Moreover, they employ the same faculty, whatever they contemplate (despite Kant's endeavour to distinguish

---

[1] *Theory* is a Greek word meaning *contemplation* or *teaching* (from θεωρέω); *practice* also is a Greek word (from πράσσω) meaning *action*. Human life is made up of *teaching* and *action*, and philosophy is a species of *teaching*, not of *action*. The phrase *practical philosophy* cannot, therefore, be taken to mean that philosophy is *active* (although that would seem to be its meaning); it can only refer to that part of teaching which deals with *action* in human life. This is more important than may appear at first sight.

the power[2] of *theoretical* reason from that of *practical* reason). The contemplative faculty is a single faculty of knowledge applied to different objects.

On what basis is philosophy divided into the two theories we have described?

As we have seen, all things which become objects of thought can be considered under two aspects, that is, either as they *are* or as they *have to be*. This appears the most obvious division of philosophy, but it is not yet that for which we are searching. What we call 'the theory of practice' does not determine how all things must be, but only how human actions have to be.

This is not an arbitrary restriction. In the last analysis, philosophy is for human beings, and it is reasonable that its divisions should be accommodated to human beings, provided always that truth is safeguarded.

3. We must note that our mind not only *knows*, up to a certain point, what beings are and how they act, but also *judges* with certainty, or on the basis of probable opinion, how they have to be and act. Very often, however, it is not in our power to make beings be or act as we judge they should; we can only consider what they have to be or do. But there are some things which we can make what we know they have to be. Such are our own actions, and our *perfection* depends upon what we do about them.

It is necessary and useful, therefore, that philosophy should have a separate section for those actions whose form we can determine, and on which our perfection depends. This division of philosophy will be dedicated to human beings,[3] and will be cut off from the great body of philosophical teaching. It will include neither theory about beings and their *de facto* activity, nor theory about how beings over which we have no influence have to be and act in order to be perfect. In a word, we exclude from this special section whatever illuminates our intellect without directing our life. We

---

[2] See my observations on Kant's distinction between theoretical and practical reason in *Opusculi filosofici* (vol. 1, p. 106, Milan 1827). It should be noted, however, that I accept an essential distinction between *theoretical* and *practical reason* (although what I call *practical reason* has no connection with Kant's practical reason). It is not the source of any part of philosophy, but the source (the efficient cause) of human actions themselves. Understood in this way, the distinction is of the greatest importance, although generally overlooked by philosophers (cf. *Principles of Ethics*, 186, 187)

[3] This does not mean that the foundations of morality are not common to all intelligent beings, but that ethics encompasses more than the fundamental elements of morals. It applies these elements to human activity; it adapts them for human use.

concentrate instead on whatever relates to the rule governing the actions of which we are authors and rulers. This rule serves as a guide directing our steps in our journey through life.

4. The reason for separating ethics from the rest of philosophy also throws light on the nature of this part of human learning. Ethics is not only theory about practice in general; it is concerned with how *we ourselves act*, and hence very different from teaching concerned with perfection in things over which we have no power. For example, I may research the elements necessary to perfection in animals, but this kind of knowledge will not be of much practical use to me. Animals depend upon nature for their perfection, not on me. The perfection of things in nature could constitute a theory about the *activity* of the supreme being, the author of nature; it can be related to his *art* and *his praxis*; but it will not regulate my own activities.

Moreover, it is not sufficient to accurately separate moral teaching from the other philosophical sciences and from all the other *theories of activity*;[4] it is not sufficient to assign moral philosophy its own sphere and delineate its limits. If an *activity* or *art* is a habit of acting according to certain norms for the sake of achieving an end, every *art* belongs to practice and is practice; every science, on the contrary, is theory. But the theory of every activity can be investigated and in this way coincides with moral teaching as a *theory of practice* and of human practice when human activity is in question. And all activity, of course, in so far as it is exercised by human beings, lies within human power. The theory of painting, of sculpture, and of every cultural and technical activity serves, in fact, as a guide to human actions. How then can ethics be the sole guide of these actions, and how does it differ in its application from other sciences concerned with activities proper to human beings?

5. The difference between ethics and other guides to human action is immense, and provides complete justification for the claim that ethics is the sole guide and regulator of human actions. It is, of course, true that the rules of painting, architecture and other activities have to be followed by those wishing to be good painters, good architects and in general *good artists*, but they do not have to be followed by those who wish to be *good humans*. What makes a painter good, and what makes a human being good are obviously different. An excellent painter can be a bad man or woman, and a good man or woman can be a bad painter. The purpose of ethics,

---

[4] Scientific ethics is also the theory of an activity, that is, of the art of right living.

however, is to make human beings good; the science of painting is directed to forming good painters. Human beings are good when their actions are good and as such governed by what is upright and just. The painter is good as painter not when his actions are good in themselves as human actions, but when some of his actions, his painting actions, are good relative only to painting walls or canvases and so on.

6. The differences, therefore, between morality and the human activities we have mentioned can be listed as follows: 1st, morality renders human actions good; other activities only render human actions suitable for obtaining some effect — a statue, a machine, something manufactured — exterior to human beings. What is good about these actions is not found in the actions themselves, but in what has been produced and relative to what has been produced. 2nd, morality makes actions good in so far as they are human (their intended goodness); other activities make actions good relative to the effect they produce and to the effort made to produce them, not relative to the final intention for which the acts are done. 3rd, moral good consequently extends to all human actions, and is essentially the same in them all. But good relative to certain activities is extended only to the single complexes of actions making up the different activities, in each of which the goodness or rather the *suitability* of the actions differs according to the object of the art.

7. What has been said helps to clarify the intimate nature of the moral sciences. At the same time, it prompts a clearer understanding of the limits proper to these sciences. As we have seen, ethics has a special place in the great body of philosophical learning. Its supreme importance and dignity lies in its capacity for teaching how to make human actions and their authors good. This is all-important. If we ourselves are evil, the goodness of other things, including our possessions, is irrelevant. This is why the study of morality has a special position as the greatest and ultimate branch of learning. Infinite knowledge is useless if finally it does not help us improve ourselves.

Thinking is only the first step to action. We do not improve as a result of simple contemplation, but as a consequence of *willing* activity. The will is the apex of the human person; when the will is good, the human person is good. But if sciences and activities improve the human person only in so far as they improve the will, and if learning is of supreme importance to human beings relative to the improvement of the will alone, a distinction must be made between the sciences and activities that assist human perfection only indirectly and remotely, and the uniquely noble science that indicates the norms of voluntary activity which, in perfecting the good will, make us good and perfect.

8. However, the exact outline of ethics can be determined still further. There is no doubt that goodness and human perfection are the sole good of human beings; there can be no good for human beings which does not leave them better than they were. It is also certain that the actuation of human perfection depends upon the observance of the norms discovered by ethical science, the definition of which includes human perfectibility. Nevertheless, a problem arises. Do the norms which improve and perfect human beings have a value independently of human beings? A careful examination of this important and difficult question leads to the conclusion that the need to obey upright and just norms does not spring from the realisation that we perfect ourselves in this way. Human perfection is the effect of obedience, not its reason. The obligation we have of conforming to the requirements of uprightness and justice is simple, immediate and absolute; it is independent of any consideration about the effects of such conformity in the person who acts; it is an authority whose very presence reveals the rule of uprightness. Of itself, this rule requires the highest reverence that cannot be gainsaid whatever the outcome. We have to conclude therefore (to our surprise, perhaps) that *what can be taught about human perfection* as the effect of virtue, differs from *moral teaching*. The latter is authoritative and powerful in its own right, and strictly independent of human perfection to which it communicates its own splendour. Hence the origin of two distinct, but closely related sciences: *ethics*, and the science of human perfection.

9. The sciences of *human perfection* and *eudaimonology* (the science of human happiness) are practically speaking the same thing. When analysed, *human happiness* and *human perfection* more or less coincide. It will not be necessary for me to distinguish them. For the moment I can speak of them indifferently. But I do have to describe briefly the general elements of the science of human perfection which either already form the basis of special sciences or are sure to do so in the future.

Human perfection can be considered in *individuals* or in *society*. In both cases, the fundamental problems are: 1st, what is the concept (nature) of human perfection? 2nd, what are the means for achieving human perfection, and what are the degrees by which it is approached and reached? Research into these problems gives rise to the following sciences (besides *ethics* which deals with the *cause* of human perfection).

I. *Telethics*, which is concerned with human perfection, and *eudaimonology* which is concerned with human happiness. These sciences are dedicated to expounding the *concept* or essence of human perfection and human happiness. Note that human perfection and human happiness are located only in *individuals*.

II. *Ascetics*, which is concerned with the means by which the *individual* can draw near to and educate himself in virtue and perfection.

III. *Pedagogics*, which is concerned with the means or art by which other *individuals* can be attracted to and educated for perfection.

IV. *Economics*, which is concerned with the government of the family, or the art of governing the family so as to lead the *individuals* composing it to human perfection and happiness. This science embraces only the means available to domestic society, and the use of power proper to the government of a family.

V. *Politics*, which is concerned with the government of states, or the art of governing civil society so as to lead the *individuals* composing it to human perfection and happiness. This science embraces only the means available to civil associations, and the use of power proper to civil government.

It is clear from our description of these sciences that the art of promoting perfection in *others* is threefold because it is concerned either with single individuals, or individuals united in family society, or individuals as members of civic society. *Domestic society* and *political society* would of course be non-existent if there were not two methods for the progressive improvement and advantage of their members. Without these methods, government of the family and the state would be aimless and vain.

All these sciences, therefore, must be distinguished from ethics. Special attention must be given to this distinction in the case of the sciences closest to ethics and most like it because ethics, with its absolute exigency, has its own place superior to every other branch of philosophy. Its object is not humanity or some other limited nature, but eternal, unshakeable truths requiring unconditional respect and obedience. Such truths are independent of reasons extrinsic to themselves; the respect we owe them is based upon a simple, irrefutable, evident reason shining in them and impervious to exceptions, ignorance, contradiction and violence of any sort.

10. Nevertheless, ethics is still confused with the other sciences we have mentioned, especially with eudaimonology. In modern times sensism, after invading European culture, has ensured the substitution of ethics by eudaimonology, and it would be useful to

see how this has come about. To do this adequately we would have to refer to the theory of beings as they are. Ethics is a corollary of this theory, and dependent upon it in such a way that every ethical error has its corresponding mistake in the theory. An examination of the history of ethics, however, will be sufficient to illustrate how the eudaimonological sciences have invaded and overrun the territory of moral science.

Francesco Maria Zanotti's *Moral Philosophy according to the Peripatetics — a Compendium* was fairly well known in Italy during the last century when the complete absorption of morals by eudaimonology was underway. The book gives us a clear idea of what was taking place, and how the same process had already been effected in classical Greek philosophy. Aristotle is to Epicurus as Zanotti is to Gioia.

Zanotti first presents *happiness* as the final end of human beings, and attempts to prove that it consists in an amalgam of pleasure, *virtue* and contemplation, that is, an amalgam of what is good and proper to human nature. We may note in passing that here the concept of virtue is still distinct from that of happiness. According to Zanotti, *happiness* is the end, and *virtue* one means amongst several of attaining happiness. As it stands, eudaimonology has not yet absorbed ethics entirely, but it is easy to see that the two sciences are about to be confused. If ethics has virtue for its object, why use happiness as a starting point and describe happiness at such length? The first words of the book show that the true subject of the work has already been lost to sight. This is inevitable if virtue is simply a means to happiness. In this case, it cannot have an *absolute*, but only a *relative* value, and indeed only a relative existence. Even here, however, there is an obvious contradiction: virtue could not be a means to happiness if it were not first something in itself. Nothing cannot be a means to anything. Ethics must first tell us what virtue is in itself, and then show how it is a means to human happiness. Zanotti, however, follows Aristotle by immediately asserting that virtue is a means to happiness, while neglecting to investigate the meaning of virtue in itself. In a word he ignores the essential question of ethics: 'What is virtue in itself?' And ethics, after all, is the science which has virtue as its subject.

When philosophical schools have gone so far as to forget the essential question of ethics and consider virtue only as relative to happiness and as a means to happiness, we can be sure that moral science is near collapse. In forgetting the essence of virtue, human ingenuity is preparing itself for an immediate denial of this essence. It is easy to move from: 'Virtue is a means to happiness' to 'Virtue is only the means to happiness'. The first formula obliterates virtue, the second denies its existence. Happiness alone, and the means to happiness, are the sole elements of ethics when philosophy reaches final corruption; eudaimonology has eliminated ethics.

11. Having considered the genuine nature and limits of ethics, we must now examine briefly its natural division.

This division must be deduced and justified, not simply asserted. We must therefore analyse the nature and definition of our science, using what has already been said about the quality and sphere of ethics to discover its correct division and order.

We have defined ethics as: 'the science that brings together in orderly fashion the norms according to which human actions have to be regulated, and that illustrates the relationship between these actions and their norms.' But human actions are present to the mind either in their individual existence, furnished with their own factual circumstances, or classified in species and more or less restricted genera. Moral norms, therefore, need to correspond to individual, realised actions or to classified actions. In this way, *generic* norms will regulate generic classes of action, *specific* norms specific classes, and particular norms will forbid or permit particular, real actions. Ethics, defined as the science 'bringing together moral laws or norms', will naturally be set out in such a way that more general rules covering all actions come first, to be followed by laws restricted to lesser complexes of actions, and finally by rules of conduct for particular cases. In addition, there must be a common form for all moral norms, whatever their extension. In other words, because they are moral, these norms must indicate and prescribe what is *morally good* in all actions.

Moral formulas, therefore, can be brought together under one heading, whatever aspect they present, because they are determined by the end to which they all tend. This heading is a supreme formula: 'Do what is morally good, and avoid moral evil.' This comprises the whole of ethics which has no other aim in all its formulas and laws than promoting moral good and forbidding moral evil.

Prior to all norms and laws, therefore, whatever their extension, we find a universal principle from which lesser expressions of law are deduced as applications and consequences of the first principle. For instance, when I say: 'Do not harm your neighbour', I am stating an application or consequence of the universal law, 'Flee moral evil'. Moreover, this universal norm is the reason underlying all its consequences and applications. If I am asked why I should not harm my neighbour, I can only answer: 'Because it is morally bad to do so.' On the other hand, if I am asked why I should avoid moral evil, only an explanation of the meaning of *moral evil* will show that such evil is to be avoided.

All laws, therefore, are reduced to the universal norm from which they descend, which evidently explains them, and which clearly indicates their necessity. Reasoning about this final, universal law has only a single aim: to state the *essence of morality* (the nature of moral good and evil). As soon as this essence has been known and considered, that is, as soon as the meaning of *moral good and evil* has been grasped, the force of obligation, present in the whole of moral legislation, makes itself felt. Ethics exists simply to manifest moral good which of itself is clearly authoritative.

Ethics has to begin, therefore, by clearly stating the elements that constitute the essence of morality. Until this has been achieved, the deduction of moral laws and norms is impossible. They would be blind, gratuitous assertions, without the backing of the clear authority and necessity present in the good they seek to prescribe for human activity. The essence of morality, considered reflectively by human beings and clearly enunciated, is therefore what we call the *principle of ethics*.

It follows that the first, natural division in moral science is between pure and applied ethics. *Pure ethics* considers the moral principle and all the conditions of its application; *applied ethics* actually applies the law to different complexes of human actions, and deduces the various categories of moral norms.

12. Each of these two main branches of ethics is subdivided into the following principal subdivisions.

Pure ethics obviously has three parts, each concerned with a matter of great importance. The first deals with the principle of ethics, the source of obligation and the origin of laws;[5] the second with the condition of the subject to whom the principle must be applied; the third with the manner of applying the principle. If we wished to distinguish them by name, they could be called: pure nomology, moral anthropology and moral logic.

---

[5] The *moral principle* or supreme law cannot be considered in isolation. It must be seen in its essential relationship with the subject (the human being) which, when acting, either conforms to it or turns away from it. In itself the *moral principle* is the *essential law*, the possibility of moral good or evil; in the subject, the moral principle is *moral good* or *evil* itself. Ethics, therefore, requires two sections, one dealing with the *supreme moral law*, the other with the *moral good* or *evil* present in the subject as a result of observance or non-observance of the law.

It is clear that all three parts are equally essential to pure ethics. The first establishes the supreme law which, however, remains sterile until applied to human beings, for whom ethics is intended. But this cannot be achieved without some knowledge of human beings as subjects of moral good and evil. There can be no development of the law without knowledge of the conditions in which it is to be applied nor without knowledge of human beings as subjects of obligation in their meritorious or demeritorious relationship with moral good and evil. Finally, we need moral logic in order to avoid error when we deduce other laws from the supreme law, and to clarify rules enabling us to reason correctly in applying the principle of ethics to the human subject, especially in difficult situations.

The works that we are publishing in this collection will cover these three areas of pure ethics. *Principles of Ethics* and *An Anthropology in Aid of Moral Science* are dedicated respectively to *nomology* and *moral anthropology*; *Conscience*, which deals with a very intricate question confused by incessant controversy, is of supreme importance for a good life and forms the principal part of *moral logic*.

13. In applied ethics, which deduces moral laws in their order of generality from the highest to the most particular, subdivisions depend upon the consideration of laws in themselves or in the subject in whom their force is manifest when he obeys or neglects them. The primary subdivision of applied ethics, therefore, should be concerned with the *formation of moral laws or formulas* (in themselves), on the one hand, and with the *execution of moral laws or formulas* (in the subject), on the other. These are two convenient titles to which all moral matters may be reduced.[6]

14. The general divisions of ethics, therefore, may be set out as follows:

I

Pure Ethics

Part 1. Pure nomology which considers the supreme law or principle of ethics.
Part 2. Moral anthropology which considers the human, moral subject in the natural order.
Part 3. Moral logic which considers the manner of applying the *moral principle* to the *moral subject* without danger of error, and the way to deduce lesser laws and formulas.

[6] The study of moral habits, e.g. the study of *virtues* and *vices*, has its place in the second part of applied ethics which considers laws or moral formulas in the subject who carries them out.

II

Applied ethics

Part 1. Derived moral laws or formulas, considered in themselves.

Section 1. Formulas regarding the supreme intelligent being: duties towards *God*.

Section 2. Formulas regarding the human intelligent being: duties towards the *human subject*.

    Chapter 1. Duties towards the *human subject* in general.

    Chapter 2. Duties towards the *human subject* arising from special relationships:

        A. the relationship a human subject has with himself (duties towards oneself);

        B. relationships in a family;

        C. relationships in political society;

        D. relationships in moral or religious society;

        E. special contracts or pacts, etc.

Part 2. Moral laws or formulas considered in the subject who carries them out.

Section 1. The *active principle* who carries out the moral formulas.

    Chapter 1. Moral acts (the nature of moral acts, imputation of merit, etc.).

    Chapter 2. Moral habits (virtues and vices).

Section 2. The *means* which help the subject to carry out the laws.

Section 3. The *effect* brought about in the moral subject by adherence to or neglect of moral laws (the relationship between *virtue* and *happiness*).

Contents

CHAPTER 1

The first moral law

Article 1. Moral law in general	3
Article 2. The first moral law	6
Article 3. The principle of ethics is placed in human beings by nature	9
Article 4. The first moral law in itself and in its subject	12

CHAPTER 2

The idea of being as the supreme rule for judging about good in general

Article 1. The nature of good	16
Article 2. The nature of evil	30
Article 3. The idea of being is the notion with which we make judgments about good in general	31

CHAPTER 3

The idea of being as the principle of eudaimonology

Article 1. Definition of eudaimonology	33
Article 2. The idea of being is the principle of eudaimonology	33
Article 3. Subjective good	34
Article 4. The principle underlying eudaimonology	36
Article 5. The good of existence and the good of perfection	37
Article 6. The evil of deterioration and the evil of destruction	38
Article 7. Absolute good	39
Article 8. Happiness	41
Article 9. The dignity of the intelligent subject	44

CHAPTER 4

The idea of being as the principle of ethics

Article 1. Summary	46
Article 2. Objective good	47
Article 3. The relationship between objective and subjective good	49
Article 4. The relationship between objective and absolute good	51
Article 5. Objective good is the source of moral good, subjective good the source of good as well-being	51
Article 6. Moral good is the work of the will	54
Article 7. The order in moral good	55
Article 8. Morally good acts always have the good of intelligent being as their end, and tend to the absolute	59
Article 9. The twofold dignity of moral good	61
Article 10. Moral legislation expressed more perfectly	62

CHAPTER 5

The will as the cause of moral good and evil

Article 1. The nature of the will	64
Article 2. Free will reveals itself as human beings reflect	65
Article 3. How actions and affections depend upon free will	68
Article 4. The principle of justice consists in ACKNOWLEDGING the being we know	79
Article 5. Truth is the principle of morality	82
Article 6. How the force of obligation is made known within us	83
Article 7. An objection overcome	85
Article 8. Corollaries about freedom of the will	87

CHAPTER 6

The powers involved in moral acts

Article 1. Moral powers in themselves and by participation	88
Article 2. Moral intellect	88
Article 3. Moral reason	88
Article 4. Eudaimonological reason	89
Article 5. Practical reason	89

Article 6. Moral reason is the source of every law except the first 90
Article 7. The definition of conscience 90

CHAPTER 7

The two elements of moral acts

Article 1. Law and will as the two elements of moral acts 92
Article 2. The imputability of acts 92
Article 3. The distinction between sin and fault 93
Article 4. Moral goodness is 'productive' and 'perfective' 94
Article 5. Gratitude 95
Article 6. Moral goodness as 'perfective' 96
Article 7. Duties with a corresponding right in those towards whom the duties are exercised 98
Article 8. Duties towards oneself 99

PRINCIPLES OF ETHICS

Saepe audisti BONI IDEAM *esse maximam disciplinam.* [You have often been told that the IDEA OF THE GOOD is the supreme directive.] (Plato, *Republic*, 6)

PRINCIPLES OF ETHICS

When your eye is sound,
your whole body is full of light
(Lk 11, 34)

1

THE FIRST MORAL LAW

Article 1.
Moral law in general

1. The moral law is a notion of the mind[1] used for making a judgment about the morality of human actions, which must be guided by it.

---

[1] When I say that law is only 'a *notion* with which the mind judges', the definition of law, in my opinion, is reduced to its simplest philosophical form. However, it may not be altogether clear how law is a notion, and an example may help to clarify my thought. The moral law 'no one must harm his fellow human being' prohibits actions which harm my neighbour. Thus every time I am involved in a harmful act, the law requires me to *judge* it as forbidden. But *how* do I judge that an act is harmful to my neighbour? Clearly, I use the notion of *harm*, because otherwise I could never distinguish between useful and harmful actions, just as, if I do not have the notion of colour, I cannot differentiate green from yellow or purple from red. By comparing harmful actions with the notion of *harmfulness* as their type, I come to know which actions are harmful. A notion, therefore, is always the principle or rule of judgment.

But, it may be objected, the law that 'it is illicit to harm your fellow human being' is itself a judgment; what notion, then, am I using as a rule to make this judgment and formulate the law? I am using the notion of what is illicit. When we know what constitutes the *illicitness* of actions, we also know that harmful actions are illicit. Thus the notion of the illicitness of actions is itself the *law*. According to this law, I judge about the morality or probity of actions, noting them as licit or illicit.

This analysis of law clearly shows that laws have, so to speak, a hierarchical order, some being higher, some lower. The higher laws are more general, while the lower are more specific. Specific laws state the same

2. Three conditions are necessary for using this notion to judge human actions:

    1. The notion must have been *received* in the mind of the person judging.

    2. The subject possessing the notion must be aware of its suitability as a rule for moral judgments. This awareness *promulgates* the notion in the subject so that the notion takes on the nature and force of law.[2]

as general laws but more distinctly and explicitly. Thus the moral law 'You must not harm your fellow human being' is lower and less general than 'You must not do what is illicit'. In both these laws, expressed as propositions, there is a *notion* which the mind uses for judging whether actions are good or evil. It is, therefore, essentially law because 'law' simply means a *rule* with which to distinguish right from wrong.

This observation agrees with the common definition of law, *Lex est recta agendorum ratio* [law is the right reason of actions], because a *reason* and a *notion* are really the same thing. *Notion*, however, expresses a different relationship from *reason*, just as *idea* expresses the same thing as *notion* and *reason*, but in a different respect. This will be understood more clearly if we bear in mind the following definitions of *reason* and *notion*:

    1. I call an idea *notion* in so far as an idea makes me *note*, that is, know things. Thus the idea of harm is a notion because it allows me to note or know which actions are harmful.

    2. I call an idea *reason* in so far as I can use the idea to *reason*, that is, as a principle for drawing some consequence from things noted or known. Thus the idea of harm is a *reason*, because I use it to draw the consequence that if I act in such a way, I do harm.

It is clear then that any idea can be simultaneously a *notion* and a *reason*, because every idea is a *species* making individuals known and an *essence* on which reasonings are founded.

---

[2] It may seem at first sight that there is no difference between the *existence* or knowledge of a law in the subject and its *promulgation*. But after serious consideration we see the difference and its relevancy. In the case of positive law, it is easy to understand that a law could be legally promulgated yet remain unknown to some people. Conversely the mind of the lawgiver could be known before any law or obligation has been *promulgated* by him. However, in the case of natural law, the difference between its existence in the subject and its promulgation is not so evident; there seems to be no third element between knowledge and ignorance of this law. If we know it, it must already exist and be promulgated; if we do not know it, it is neither promulgated nor existent in us. But we have defined law as simply a notion or idea used as an exemplar for comparing and judging our actions. An *idea* is one thing, *use* of it is another. To have an idea and not know its use is not contradictory, for we certainly do not

3. The notion must be *applied* by the subject to the actions to be judged.

If therefore we are to judge the morality of actions, the law must *exist* in us, that is, be *known*, *promulgated* and *applied*. The application completes the judgment.

know all the uses, developments and consequences of our ideas. We often have principles in our minds which remain unproductive precisely because we are ignorant of their use. Indeed the accepted difference between a thinker and a non-thinker is that the former draws many more consequences than the latter from the first principles of reasoning common to both.

There is no contradiction, therefore, between our having an idea and at the same time being totally ignorant of its use in some particular relationship. And even if both the idea and the knowledge of its use existed together, they would not be the same thing. Our mind would still have to separate them by analysis.

Let us take the first idea we use for judging about the morality of actions, and let us suppose we are totally ignorant of its use as a rule for such judgments. In this case the law would exist in us because the idea itself is the law and has all the force of law. But the law itself would not be promulgated, because we would not feel the obligatory force of the idea to be used as a rule for judging moral actions good or bad. I would go even further: the force that an idea possesses to produce consequences of its own normally remains completely hidden from us if we do not have the *experience* of seeing and feeling this force in reality.

This truth is clarified in the moral system I propose, where I demonstrate that the first moral law is the notion of being. However, although all people have this notion, only a few have reflected on its ability to serve as the rule for judging about the morality of actions. It is indeed possible to reflect upon a notion without reflecting upon its use! What takes place in the order of *reflection* takes place also in the order of *direct knowledge*. We all have the direct notion of being but if we make no direct use of it, we cannot feel its force as moral law.

We can therefore accept, without any contradiction, that in the first moments of human existence the idea of being is present unaccompanied by awareness of its aptitude to serve as law. The human being begins to be aware of this aptitude only when he begins to use it, that is, with experience. The *existence of this idea*, anterior to its *use*, has been demonstrated in *The Origin of Thought* [Leominster, 1987, cf. 398-470]

The idea then is the law (as we discover afterwards by its use), known of itself to every intelligence, although its use remains unknown until the occasion to apply it presents itself. As long as this application is not actually made (the length of time is irrelevant), the law is neither promulgated nor suggested to us. Hence, the necessity of the distinction I make between the *existence* of the law in us (the natural law) and its *promulgation*.

Article 2.
The first moral law

3. It is clear that one notion sometimes depends on another more general notion, just as notions of species depend on and presuppose the notion of their genus. For example, the notion 'human' depends on and presupposes the notion 'animal'. A series of notions, however, each of which depends on a preceding notion, must end somewhere or continue to infinity; a final notion must ultimately be reached on which all others, supposing it, depend. This ultimate notion must be independent of all others; no other notion must precede it, and it must be impossible to go beyond it.

If the moral laws in our mind are simply *notions*, we must come, in a series of these notions and laws, to a *final* law. This *final* law can also be called *first* because the words 'last' and 'first' express two relationships of a single term: what is last in the series is first when the series is reversed.

4. The first law, therefore, is the first idea or notion with which we form moral judgments. But the study of ideas shows that in the human being there is an idea, preceding all others, with which all judgments are formed.[3] Granted this, it must follow that this first idea, the principle and source of all judgments, is also the principle and source of moral judgments, and hence the first moral law, the object of our present enquiry.

The human mind forms all judgments with the idea of universal being, which is innate in the human spirit as the form of intelligence. I call it the *form* of intelligence because an analysis of human thoughts shows them to be informed by it in such a way that thought is inconceivable without it. Thus any spirit devoid of it lacks intelligence. Universal being, therefore, must be the first moral law, the notion we use to produce all moral judgments.

---

[3] I have proved this basic truth in *The Origin of Thought*, where I demonstrated that the notion of being has different uses, that in these uses it becomes successively all the principles of reasoning, and that by means of these principles every other reasoning is ultimately formed. To understand how the first principles of reasoning are simply the *application of the idea of being*, see *op. cit.* 558-573 and *Certainty*, 1112 ss [Leominster 1989].

5. We note that all things and parts of things, together with their perfections, are ultimately acts of being. Being, actuated and limited in different ways, receives different names in different things. The word *being* means simply the first activity and every activity. To say something 'is', is to say it acts. Nothing is, unless it acts; it must act in order to be; what a thing does to posit and maintain its being, is an action. Thus every action is contained in the notion of being, which indicates and measures everything; without knowing what being is, we cannot 'measure' different beings, that is, 'distinguish', 'judge', or 'perceive them intellectively'. I cannot perceive any being intellectively unless I say to myself that it is a being, that is, has the activity of its being determined in a definite mode and at a definite level. I can make no judgment about it if I do not first understand what is meant by the word *being* in general, which I always pronounce in making a judgment.

6. I have explained this at much greater length in my work on the origin of ideas, to which I refer the reader. However, we still have to see how we are capable of making judgments about moral good and evil when we only have knowledge of being. Such a problem may seem strange to anyone who has never considered the matter. Obviously, if we know what universal being is, we can understand what particular beings are. But can we understand what good and moral good are, when there is apparently no connection between beings and moral actions? I need to answer this question in detail by comparing the *being* of things with moral *good* and evil, the very purpose of this book.

What has been said so far, however, should be enough to show in general that the notion under discussion fulfils the role we have described, although we may still not be able to explain *how* this comes about. Certainly, in the light of what has been said, we are not justified in rejecting such a truth simply because we cannot explain it. To reject it, we would have to reject the proofs used to show that the idea of being is the rule of all judgments,[4] or deny the definition I have given of law as a rule of moral judgments: But as long as these two

[4] *The Origin of Thought*, 398-412

points are certain, the third also must be certain: the first rule for all judgments is the first rule for moral judgments and hence the first moral law.

7. Because the idea of universal being constitutes the *light* of reason,[5] the moral law is expressed fairly well in the formula, 'Follow reason'. But it would be more accurate to say, 'In all that you do, follow the *light* of reason.' This is the most general formula in ethics and expresses the first law more accurately than 'Follow reason' because human reason is a faithful guide only if it follows its light. Reason is the faculty with which the human spirit applies the idea of being — reasoning is simply the application of the idea.[6] The human spirit, however, is fallible, and often errs when making this application. Reason therefore is fallible because it is the power of a limited, fallible spirit. On the other hand, the light of reason cannot err because it does not depend on the human spirit. Nor does the spirit acquire it by its own efforts. It is innate, breathed into the spirit by the creator. *Being*, the light illuminating the spirit and indeed making it intelligent, is absolutely unchangeable, eternal and necessary; it is the truth itself, as I have shown at length.[7] Thus it is not reason that constitutes the supreme moral law but the idea of being whose light is used by reason. When reason adheres to the light, it is accurate; when it abandons the light, it errs.

This observation alone eliminates many of the equivocations and errors of other theories, which make human beings either gods or animals. If reason, which is the power using the light, is confused with the light, it falsely takes on the excellence and infallibility of the light. Reason becomes proud and self-reliant; the human being becomes both legislator and God in the moral universe. On the other hand, to note the fallibility of reason but ignore its divine element (the idea of being) is to debase human beings by denying them a true moral state. They are either condemned to perpetual error, or to groping in the darkness for the truth they can never be certain of finding.

[5] *The Origin of Thought*, 480-482; *Certainty*, 1112-1136
[6] *Certainty*, 1040-1377
[7] *ibid.*

I cannot enlarge on these extreme errors in this brief study, but when necessary I will indicate how they are to be avoided.

Article 3.
The principle of ethics is placed in human beings by nature

8. This follows from what has been said. If the idea of being is innate and functions as supreme law, it follows that by nature we bear within our soul the seed of all morality. We have within us the first law as the principle and source of all other laws and the guide to what is right and just.

We could never acquire the principle of morality if it were not innate. But the consensus of the human race is that we do possess it even though we can obtain cognitions only from nature as felt by us, which simply presents facts, not the reasons and laws upholding the facts.

These reasons and laws cannot be received in any way in the bodily senses. Essentially unknown to the senses, they are evident only to intelligent natures. Thus we must either deny morality or acknowledge that its principle is innate. I firmly believe that those who reject the theory of being I have set out, are forced (even against their will) to make moral actions impossible.

9. This theory, which recognises a light impressed in human nature teaching it to discern good from evil, is not new nor my own discovery. It is traditional teaching, particularly in christianity but it was obscured by intellectuals of the last century who tried to free themselves from tradition. They denied the philosophical faith of their forebears, just as they sought to free themselves from the society of their own time in order to attain total independence. Teachings were rejected simply because they were ancient or popular, which are the very reasons that give them dignity and honour.

10. Before christianity, the tradition we are discussing was defended by Cicero, among many others, in the following passage: 'Wise men taught that the moral law does not originate with the learned, nor with a decree of the peoples. It is something eternal, a wisdom with authority to command and

forbid, governing the whole world.'⁸ If, then, the law cannot be acquired, we have to say, as wise men did even before Christ, that we possess it by nature.

11. In christian times the tradition is found on nearly every page of the ecclesiastical writers. The following two passages illustrate my point. St. Jerome says, 'There is a natural holiness impressed on our souls by God. It resides in the highest part of the spirit, where it judges between what is right and what is wayward.'⁹ We note that natural holiness, innate to us, is situated in our highest part; the Latin text says *in the citadel of the soul*. This expression is fully reflected in my teaching, which indicates the sublime idea of being as the first and only innate moral law. All ideas and all human thought originate from it and are informed by it. There can be no higher or stronger part of the spirit than the dwelling of the light of being, the source of intellective life, the most simple principle of all judgments, the light of reason. This is the seat of the first norm of *thoughts* and *actions*; here error is impossible. For this reason Bonaventure and other christian teachers called it appropriately the *apex of the soul*.

12. The second passage is from St. Ivo: 'We have already seen that the *idea* of what is right is placed in our minds by God, the first truth. Through this idea each of us, having only our synderesis, differentiates between what is just and unjust without any teacher, written law or judge. With this *light* God enlightens everyone coming into the world.'¹⁰

It is clear that this passage harmonises with what I am saying. St. Ivo affirms the presence in the human being of an innate *idea* through which God enlightens everyone born into the world. It is an *idea of what is right* in such a way that with

---

⁸ *Hanc video sapientissimorum fuisse sententiam, legem neque hominum ingeniis excogitatam, nec scitum aliquod esse populorum, sed aeternum quiddam, quod universum mundum regeret, imperandi, prohibendique sapientia. De Legibus*, II,

⁹ *Est in animis nostris quaedam sanctitas naturalis a Deo impressa, quae veluti in* ARCE ANIMI *residens, pravi et recti judicium exercet. Ep. ad Demetriad.* 8.

¹⁰ *Praefati sumus a Deo prima veritate insitam esse mentibus humanis* IDEAM *recti, qua justum ab injusto quilibet sine praeceptore, sine lege scripta, sine magistratu, sola sua synderesi discernit. Hac* LUCE *Deus illuminat omnem hominem venientem in hunc mundum.*

it we distinguish, without being taught, what is just from what is unjust. This is precisely my theory. The light of reason by which God enlightens everyone coming into the world, is simply a first *idea*; it does not come from our senses but is breathed into human beings by their creator; forming the light of reason in human beings, it also gauges what is right and what is wayward. All I have added is the analysis of human thoughts in order to discover the first, sublime idea from which all other ideas come. This is the human being's true light in all his cognitions. It is none other than the *idea of being*, an idea present in all other ideas as necessary for their existence; it is their formal element, unmixed with other ideas; it is the only truly simple idea, yet wonderfully fruitful in its simplicity.[11]

[11] I had been doubtful for some time whether the earlier thinkers had seen how the idea of being precedes all other ideas and is in fact the source of all the principles of thought. The first principle for Aristotle was the principle of *contradiction*, which however is posterior both to the idea of being and to the principle of *cognition*, as I call it (cf. *The Origin of Thought* 559 ss) formed directly from the idea of being. But a passage of Alexander of Hales in his exposition of Aristotle's metaphysics removed my difficulties. He gives the idea of being first place in human intellections because he saw that the idea must precede the principle of contradiction.
Aristotle investigates the characteristics of the first principle of all human reasonings and finds they are three: 1. it is more stable and more extensively known than anything else; 2. it is absolute and unconditional; 3. it is undemonstrable and given by nature. He then shows how the principle of contradiction has precisely these characteristics.
But Alexander was not satisfied; he doubted the master's opinion. 'The intellect,' he wrote, 'has two activities, one with which it *perceives*, the other with which it analyses and divides what is perceived. In both activities there is some first thing, that is, something encountered as the first term of each activity. In the first activity the first object is being, because we cannot conceive anything by this activity without having previously conceived being; being permeates and supports all concepts' (that is, being is presupposed in all concepts as their foundation). 'In the second activity the first object is the principle of contradiction' and he explains why: 'because the principle is founded in being.' He concludes: 'Hence, just as *being* is first in the intellect's first activity' (earlier thinkers called it 'understanding simple concepts'), 'the principle of contradiction is first in the second activity. Just as all simple concepts find their explanation in being, so all complex concepts find their explanation in the principle of contradiction.'
This passage clearly indicates how, absolutely speaking, the *idea of being* is the mind's first intellection, and I confess my surprise at finding being's

Article 4.
The first moral law in itself and in its subject

13. If we observe our acts of knowledge we see that the intellect, in contradistinction to feeling, perceives objectively, that is, focuses its attention on an object different from itself. In its very act of understanding, the intelligent spirit posits something different from itself, abandoning itself in order to concentrate on what is present to it. Indeed it is a condition of intellectual activity that the term of the operation is perceived as different from the one who perceives, or better, excludes the perceiver. The opposition between the person who perceives and what he perceives is such that one cannot simultaneously be the other, nor both be perceived by the same act. Hence in the very act of perception, the one who perceives is not at the same time what is perceived.

This difference or opposition that observation reveals between the perceiver, as perceiver, and what is perceived, as perceived, is real, not imaginary.[12] There is a difference

place within ideas so clearly noted and defined. Because of its importance and the noble truth it adds to Aristotle's teaching (possibly unnoticed by Alexander), I quote the passage in full in the Latin original. *Quaeret quis: utrum sit verum quod dicit Philosophus, quod hoc principium* (of contradiction) *sit radix omnium principiorum, et omnium propositionum.* He answers the question and immediately adds this explanation: *notandum est, quod duplex est operatio intellectus. Prima est qua intelligit ipsum quod quid est* (the expression *quod quid est* means the essence and idea of a thing) *et haec operatio vocatur simplicium intelligentia. Alia est operatio intellectus qua componit et dividit* (synthesis and analysis). *Et in utraque operatione est aliquod primum, quod scilicet cadit sub prima apprehensione intellectus. Illud quod est primum in prima operatione, est* ENS; *nihil enim potest concipi simplici intelligentia, nisi concipiatur ens; et hoc quia entitas se profundat infra omnes conceptus. Primum autem in secunda operatione intellectus est hoc principium: de quolibet affirmatio vel negatio* (that is, the principle of contradiction), *et hoc quia hoc principium est fundatum super ens. Unde sicut* ENS *est primum in prima operatione; ita hoc principium in secunda. In secunda enim operatione intellectus nihil potest intelligi, nisi intellecto hoc principio. Sicut enim totum et pars non potest intelligi nisi intellecto ente; ita hoc principium: omne totum est majus sua parte, non potest intelligi nisi intellecto hoc principio firmissimo. Et sic, sicut omnes conceptus simplices resolvuntur ad* ENS; *ita omnes conceptus compositi resolvuntur ad hoc principium* (Alex. of Hales, *In XII Aristotel. metaph. libros dilucidissima explanatio*, lib. IV, text. 9).

[12] Cf. *Certainty*, 1194-1208

between being as perceived and the subject who perceives. We must therefore consider being in itself and in so far as it is employed by the intelligent subject who has the notion of it.

14. Although the perceiving subject differs from the perceived object by the very nature of intellective perception, there is a certain bond, in which understanding consists, between the perceiver and what is perceived. This bond is so intimate that a single individual is formed from the two principles without either absorbing the other. Thus we see that the light of reason (being) is united with the human subject and comes to form part of human nature in such a way that without it humanity would no longer exist.[13]

Because the bond is so intimate, the twofold nature (so to speak) of the human subject, essentially intelligent and therefore essentially in possession of a universal object of his understanding, has often been overlooked. This oversight, which confuses the object essential to the intelligent subject with the subject itself, has caused many errors. What belongs only to the object is attributed to the subject, and viceversa what belongs to the object is attributed to the subject. This mistake has given rise to two erroneous systems of ethics, to which, it seems to me, all errors in moral teaching can ultimately be reduced.

15. The first erroneous system attributes to the subject what belongs to the object. I have indicated how the object (which, for me, is the supreme moral law) is endowed with divine characteristics such as immutability, eternity, universality, necessity. All these characteristics are mistakenly attributed to the human subject, who was thus divinised. Those who uphold this system speak enthusiastically of what is divine in the human being, and make the human creature a

---

[13] Those who claim that human beings are born without any notion, deprive them in reality of intelligence. They then attempt to explain that animals become human beings by means of development and education, and that this immense leap is due to acquired sensations. But without an intellective seed from which to develop, there can be no development. These thinkers deny any such seed in human beings and are forced to posit something quite incomprehensible, such as an intellect created at some totally indeterminable point of life.

law unto himself. Kant named the system *autonomy*, that is, 'law unto oneself'.[14]

16. The second erroneous system goes to the other extreme, attributing to the object, that is, to the moral law, what belongs to the subject. The human being is changeable, temporal, limited, contingent, and every effort is made to ascribe these characteristics to the moral law. Those who uphold this system would have us believe that the law is subject to continual change, just as climates, customs, education and races change. Such a system destroys all moral legislation, and has been confidently taught and diffused along with the sensist philosophy which gave it birth. It has always been rejected and opposed not only by the learned but also by the infallible instinct of christian peoples which enables them to reject every harmful teaching despite its illusory appeal and their own lack of sophistication.

There was a time, it seems, when all philosophy was dominated by these two excessive systems. Kant posited no new system when he spoke of *heteronomy*, that is, law received from outside ourselves, in opposition to his own system of *autonomy*. He was simply pointing to the system which maintains that even moral notions are generated in us by the use of our external senses.

17. Among moral systems, therefore, that make the moral law originate from a principle outside or different from us, we must carefully distinguish between that which makes morality arise from sensations, and that which posits in the human being a principle different from the human being but intimately united with him by a law of nature. Morality dependent on sensations is false, fruitless and destructive of internal morality. Morality dependent upon an object is true, and begins by observing the internal construction of our intellectual and moral nature from which it deduces the whole

---

[14] Even St. Paul says that the Gentiles, deprived of written law, 'are a law for themselves' (Rom 2. 14), meaning the natural law. The expression has its truth in the union by which the *light* of reason and the *human being* are one indivisible thing, and cannot be understood otherwise. It excludes the system we oppose which says that the subject (the human being) and the object (being) do not remain individuals in the union but become indistinguishably one.

series of other moral laws connected with, and indicating, the marvellous, supreme principle which, shining in the soul, naturally enjoys an evident eternal stability and consistency. Against this principle no force, created or uncreated, can prevail; every finite intelligence must obey it; divinity itself, as Bossuet says, obeys it.

18. Careful consideration of the two systems we are examining shows their defective observation. Because both overlook and forget an element of human nature, their observation is necessarily imperfect. The first system, which divinises the human being, does not give enough attention to the nature of the spirit. As we have seen, the spirit is merely passive relative to the moral law; it receives the law, it does not form it. It is a subject who cannot refuse the law, not a lawgiver imposing the law.[15] On the other hand the second system completely loses sight of the striking characteristics of the moral law which are not deduced by reasoning but observed directly as facts. That is why Locke and others who uphold this system deny the irresistible force of the law. But the law binds both the person who fulfils it and the person who violates it; with invincible authority, it is unchangingly present to all human beings.

19. Between these two systems, however, which fail because of deficient observation, there is a third, founded on complete, unbiased observation. This system does not confine itself arbitrarily to deducing everything from the subject, nor does it so concentrate on the excellence of the law that it forgets the properties of the spirit which perceives the law.º It considers both subject and object and the wonderful way in which, because their properties remain separate and distinct, they form one thing without losing their identity. It affirms that, just as all obligatory force comes from the object, so feeling and awareness of feeling comes from the subject.

---

[15] *Neque enim creatura legem tribuit, sed accipit, et servat acceptam.* Ambrose, *Hexam.* 1.

2
THE IDEA OF BEING AS THE SUPREME RULE FOR JUDGING ABOUT GOOD IN GENERAL

20. After this long but necessary digression, we must return to our main topic. I have already shown how the notion of being can serve as the moral law or notion enabling us to determine what is right and what is wayward.

But *how* is the idea of being the supreme moral law; *in what way* is it the supreme rule or criterion with which we judge the morality of human actions? Working methodically, I shall begin by showing how the notion of being can be used for judging about *good* in general. Then we shall see how it can be used for judging about *moral good*. But to do this, I must first investigate the nature of good.

Article 1.
The nature of good

21. Let us start from the definition of good provided by common sense. It forms part of ordinary speech, and is doubted by no one. After the analysis and separation of its components, their systematic reunion will give us the philosophical definition of good we are seeking.

Everybody speaks of good as 'that which is *desired*'. It is impossible to call good what is detested. Good, therefore, is anything that moves enjoyably the faculty of desire which draws us to enjoy good. Everyone agrees about this. There is no need to demonstrate the absurdity of the contrary. For people in general, good means *a relationship between things and the faculty of desire*. But what are the things we call good because they can move our desire? Answering this question will lead us to a fuller, more precise notion of good.

22. A thing is good in so far as it is desired. But this implies the existence of a being capable of desire. There could be no notion of good without such a being, because a *relationship* — and good, as we have said, is a relationship between things and that which desires them — cannot be thought without the two terms of the relationship. Such a being, however, must

first desire its own existence and preservation and everything else that can make it more perfect and complete. A being with a faculty of desire employed solely in hating itself, that is, desiring nothing except self-destruction, is meaningless. No being can be in perpetual conflict with itself.

23. Careful examination of the faculty of desire reveals it as that by which a being strives to enjoy the *perfection* or enhancement the being receives or has received. This is the sole concept people have of it. In it there is also understood, and taken for granted, the tendency to delight in oneself, and to love oneself with all that is good and perfect in one's nature. Even the enjoyment itself is something good for the person experiencing it.

24. But let us consider more carefully the expression 'enjoying the perfections of one's own nature.' We distinguish between the perfection enjoyed and the enjoyment itself. There are two elements, therefore, contained in the common definition 'Good is that which is desired': first, the *enjoyment*, and second, the *perfection* enjoyed. We cannot doubt the real distinction between these two parts of good.

Common sense, when it says 'Good is that which is desired', raises a question about the two elements of good: are both necessary or is one sufficient for constituting the concept of good? When I speak of what is perfect in a nature, do I not include and posit all that is good prior to any faculty of desire? Are not grades of perfection and good assigned even to inanimate and insensitive natures? Do we not usually say that all things are good, considered in their nature? It would seem that common sense normally gives the same meaning to *perfection* and to *good*, and mentally conceives the perfections in different natures as good independently of the subject that feels them or desires them with its feeling.

Before answering this question, however, I must prepare the ground by answering another: would we have the idea of perfection if we had no faculty of desire?

25. First of all, let me point out that it is not my intention to confuse the faculty of *desire* and fruition with the faculty of *knowing*. I accept these two faculties as essentially different. I am aware that it is possible to know what is good without enjoying or even desiring it. I realise we can know the

existence of things which are good but not good for us, although good for other beings. Thus, we can form the concept of some good things without ever having experienced them. But I am asking whether we could ever have the notion of good if we had never felt or desired any good. And to avoid any misunderstanding of the word *desire*, I repeat that I take it to mean the faculty of tending to certain things in order to enjoy them, a faculty presupposing and intimately united with the faculty of feeling pleasure in the perfections in different natures.

Those acquainted with my theory on the origin of human knowledge will realise immediately that I must answer negatively. If we had never experienced the pleasure of the perfections of our own or another nature, we could not form the idea of a perfection in any nature. It is obvious that there is no other way for a feeling being to perceive the perfections of its own nature except by feeling them. Nor can the intellect think something as good, unless feeling first presents it.[16] Let us now return to the first question.

26. It is impossible, therefore, to perceive or *know* what is good and perfect in different natures, without feeling and desiring it, but are feeling and desire necessary for the *existence* of what is good and perfect? In other words, can what is perfect and good *exist* without its being feelable and therefore desirable?

In order to know that something is a perfection, we must know it is acceptable to the nature which possesses it or to which it is referred. But it cannot be acceptable unless it is feelable in some way; perfections do not exist for a being that does not feel. A being without sensation does not exist to itself but only to that which feels it.[17] Only the one who feels himself exists to himself. The annihilation of feeling is the annihilation of the relationship between the individual's nature and the individual. In short, where there is no feeling, there is no 'myself', and certainly no *subject*.

[16] The explanation of the way *sense* presents to the *understanding* the things to be perceived has been treated at length by me in *The Origin of Thought* [630-1019]. Cf. also *Opuscoli Filosofici*, vol. 1 [Milan, 1828].

[17] In my opinion this observation is of great importance but difficult to explain. Because we are endowed with feeling, we tend to posit feeling in

The idea of being and good in general

This observation seems to me to be very important. It is the starting point for understanding correctly my train of thought. I affirm that natures without any sensitivity whatsoever are entirely neutral and indifferent to their own grade of perfection, from existence upwards. Thus, their existence and other properties called perfections are such only relatively to the being (whatever it may be) that feels and desires them, or contemplates them as desired or desirable by other beings. We must conclude that if the existence of insensitive matter, with its nature and perfections, could not be felt or mentally conceived by some other being, these qualities could never be called perfections, and would never be known as such. Indeed, deprived of the ability to be felt, they would not even *be*, because they could not be mentally conceived if their capacity for being the matter of feeling were removed. The perfections of inanimate things exist and are known only because of their connection with some faculty of feeling and desire, although these faculties of feeling and desire are outside them, located in another being.

---

inanimate things. Generally we base the ideas of things on the idea we have of ourselves. Even when we do not expressly and directly attribute feeling to things, we tend to conceive them mentally as something in themselves. But their existence is only relative to the person feeling it or contemplating it as felt. It is very difficult to form the idea of inanimate things relative to themselves. It is even more difficult to dismiss the vague, false idea formed by our imagination that they are something. But we must rid ourselves of such imaginary ideas. For instance, let us imagine that all thought and feeling have ceased in us. We would have no idea of ourselves; we would cease to exist to ourselves. The nothingness of insensitive things is a fact, but even in this respect they must be excluded from our imagination so that no illusory idea remains to become a source of innumerable errors. We will be left therefore with an objective existence of inanimate things, that is, relative solely to the being to which they become object or at least term of action.

Some thinkers, like Plato, noticed this purely relative existence of material things and consequently denied their true existence. Others, like the idealists, especially in Germany, tried to make them part of the spirit. In my system I keep solely to observation, limiting myself to the fact that 'a force exists modifying us and producing sensations. And in so far as it modifies us we affirm its existence.' This force is a body. A body is also a substance in so far as the first idea that we have of a body stands by itself, that is, a body is conceived without the need of another being to which it adheres. It is this characteristic which marks subordinate, created substances. Cf. *Origin of Thought*, 630 ss.

The perfection of a flower, for example, or of a fruit, is in the flower and the fruit. But it is 'myself', a being different from the flower and the fruit, who desires and experiences the scent of the flower and the taste of the fruit. It is I who form the idea of the fruit and the flower, of their nature, their perfections, that is, of what belongs or does not belong to their nature. This connection, then, which the flower and fruit have with me, and generally with beings capable of receiving sensations from them, is so essential that their existence presupposes the connection. If we imagine the annihilation of this connection with a desiring subject, we have removed and annihilated the beings themselves, along with their possibility.

27. This analysis I have made of perfections in natures without feeling indicates that *sense*, either in the being possessing the perfection or in some entirely different being, is required for the idea of a *perfection* of any nature. A perfection is called 'perfection' and is such precisely because of its relationship with sense; if we reject its ability to be felt, its concept no longer remains. When I say *ability to be felt*, I mean the ability the perfection has to be felt and desired by anyone at all.

There is therefore a strict, essential relationship and connection between the *perfection* of a nature and the *desire* for the same. Sentient desire is a necessary condition for the existence of this perfection. *Good* cannot be formed from one element alone; *perfection* and *sense* are relative terms. This fact, extraordinary as it may seem, is irrefutable because given by the analysis of the concept of perfection. A perfection which gives no enjoyment cannot be conceived as a perfection; it is something indifferent, perfecting nothing because it is nothing.

Nevertheless, despite the essential relationship and connection between *perfection* and *feeling* in natures, we must recognise and establish their difference, which is also essential. Although the two elements are truly and inseparably united, so that one embraces the other, and the idea of one includes the idea of the other, they are not the same. Their relationship is that of *opposites*, in such a way that they cannot be intermingled or identified with each other.

28. Sense, desire, enjoyment cannot be mentally conceived without matter that is felt, desired and enjoyed. But the concept is not so bound to the actual feeling of matter that we cannot think of matter as existing even outside the act in which it is felt and enjoyed. However, if it is outside the act, it must be conceived as potentially feelable and enjoyable: if not, its concept disappears together with any thought of it. The concept, therefore, of the matter of enjoyment (called 'perfection') does not contain any actual desire for it. It remains something distinct from our act of enjoyment, and from the actual pleasing sensation we have of it.[18]

29. On the one hand perfection in natures presupposes some sense-faculty and can only be understood to exist as feelable; on the other, its concept indicates an independent subsistence that can produce enjoyment without receiving existence from it. Thus, whenever we attempt to consider perfections in different natures by themselves and not as felt, they cannot be thought and no longer exist; considered as united with the enjoyment they produce they not only exist but exist in an absolute way, independently of any sensation referred to them. This extraordinary union and difference between *perfection* in a nature and *feeling* of the nature originate simultaneously and inseparably in an unchangeable order, the first as generating, the second as generated.[19]

After this discussion on *perfections* in natures and their *enjoyment*, I can now ask whether these perfections are something good in themselves, independently of being felt, and whether common sense is correct in seeing good in non-sensitive, inanimate natures.

---

[18] I do not need to discuss how, in the phenomenon of sensation, we conceive some matter different from and independent of sensation itself. Anyone acquainted with my teaching about sensations in *The Origin of Thought* [722 ss] will be able to follow this important investigation and understand how the concept of some matter of sensation remains in our mind and differs from sensation itself by means of the subjective and extra-subjective forms of feeling. In extra-subjective feeling, sensations are reproduced identically according to determined laws, which presuppose an agent of which we know only its power to modify our feeling.

[19] This order of opposition, that is, of simultaneous union and distinction, is found in all beings *mentally conceived*. Possible things (ideas) do not exist outside the mind; they cannot be conceived unrelated to an

30. First, the word 'perfection' expresses an essential relationship with possible enjoyment of the perfection. Common sense is correct when it sees all perfections as good, even perfections of non-sensitive, inanimate things, because these perfections have all the conditions necessary for good. Their good is an endowment of the natures possessing it and pleases its perceiver, whether the latter is the same or some other nature.

31. There is an important consequence regarding the different kinds of good we have indicated. We have dealt with what is good and is felt as desirable by the one who possesses the good; we have also spoken about what is good and is felt as good by others but not by its own non-sentient possessor. Now such kinds of good differ according to the different existence of the beings themselves. In a word, *beings are good in so far as they are.*

Beings lacking sense-activity certainly differ from those that feel. Non-sensitive beings, as we have said, do not exist to themselves nor feel themselves, nor do they understand. Thus they are not a good to themselves. Relative to themselves, all their perfections are nothing because what is not felt or understood is nothing. Here we must be careful to avoid arbitrary suppositions. For example, to attribute some kind of feeling to material beings is to put them in the class of feeling beings, which is contrary to our supposition about the category of beings we are considering. We must not forget that words, like 'body' for example, are given to things in so far as we know them, and signify the (known) essence of a thing (essence is precisely what is understood in the idea of the thing). According to the hypothesis and definition, therefore, inanimate bodies are non-sensitive. Furthermore, even if everything we knew possessed feeling, the distinction between perfection in a nature and sensation would still exist.

intelligence, just as it is impossible to conceive an intelligent being without them. However, although these two essences originate immediately and simultaneously when they unite in one individual, they nevertheless originate with an order between them. Thus possible things emerge as independent, absolute, necessary, eternal, active; the mind originates passively and as an effect of possible things — we are speaking of course of a mind belonging to a contingent, changeable, fallible being. Cf. *Certainty*, 1457-1460.

The bond intimately uniting the two essences, which are seen by reason as both united and distinct at one and the same time and mutually conditioning one another, would also exist. We must conclude that non-sensitive nature (whether united individually or not to feeling) is ordered to sense, whose matter it supplies. In and through sensation, non-sensitive nature provides the object of intelligence,[20] and depends for its definition on being both this object and the matter of feeling. Perfections in a feeling nature, therefore, are good in so far as that nature exists. They are good considered relatively (to the feeling) on the one hand, and independently (in themselves) on the other. Let us clarify and develop this truth.

32. Immaterial beings, and more generally, natures with their perfections, do not exist unless they are felt, whether feeling is intimately and individually united with them or not. This means they depend on feeling for their existence; without this relationship they are neither possible nor thinkable. If they do in fact exist, they can do so only on condition they are independent and productive of feeling through which they act as authors of knowledge. Feeling on the other hand exists only as something produced, as an effect, as something experienced. In other words, for perfections in natures to be *possible*, they must be related to feeling; to be *subsistent*, they must be independent of feeling. This contrast will not surprise us if we note how often it is present in other cases. Indeed it is the law and universal form of the relationships between *subsistences* and *possibilities*, between things and ideas. In the last analysis it constitutes the essential means enabling our intelligence to pass from one thing to another. For example, we cannot think of the idea of cause without simultaneously thinking of the correlative idea of effect. Cause is here dependent on and conditioned by effect, but only in the order of possibility and ideas. In the order of real things and subsistences the opposite is true: a really subsistent cause subsists independently of its effect, even though the latter is conditioned by and dependent on the cause. The conditions for the *ideal order* therefore vary from and are

---

[20] The difference between the *matter* of feeling and the *object* of intelligence is explained in the *Origin of Thought*, 1005-1019.

even opposed to those of the *real order*. Thus, although the perfections in things and consequently all good in them are mentally seen as dependent on feeling, they are in their real existence conceived as causes of feeling, not effects, and independent of these effects.

Let us try now to explain further the nature of good, and perfect its definition.

33. To analyse the *concept* of good means analysing an object of our understanding, because a *concept* is always an object of understanding. What then does our understanding notice in the concept of good? We have seen that: 1. perfections in things always have a hidden connection with desire; 2. the understanding sees the perfections as independent and devoid of this connection. As independent, these perfections need to be subjected to further analysis which will provide new results. Omission of words like 'feeling' and 'desire' does not mean they are not present and understood. Whenever I say 'perfection', I mean all that is needed to constitute perfection. The word, therefore, implicitly contains perfection's essential but sometimes remote connection with feeling.

34. It is a law of the intellect that it 'forgets or at least no longer adverts to what it posited in its concepts at the moment of forming them.' Concepts are retained in a synthetic state, rather like a formula or code for what was originally seen but is now referred to generally without specific attention. Algebraic calculations are a very good example of this process. The conditions of the problem determine the symbols and first equation. The conditions are then ignored and each step carried out according to particular rules without advertence to the reasoning behind them. But the result is true because the *signs* of the reasoning are always retained and, when desired, allow the reasoning to be clearly and distinctly recalled.[21]

---

[21] This *observation* gave rise to *nominalism* (all errors begin with some truth incorrectly used). Nominalists fail to notice that the intellect could not use *numbers* without giving them some *general* value. It is only the specific, determined value that the intellect forgets when using numbers. When we reason using numbers, we always retain those relationships and data which allow us to indicate their determined value. These data and relationships constitute the general value of numbers. Clearly, this fact, far

In the same way, investigation of the *origin* of our ideas of perfections in things reveals that: 1. we first associated pleasant feelings with these perfections, because, for us, perfection means pleasant impressions taking place or being anticipated either in us or in some other sensitive being; 2. we then attributed the concept of *perfection* to the things we experienced pleasantly, but now without paying attention to their capacity to modify us or any other being. In this case the word 'perfection' comes to mean something in itself, independent of the feeling to which it was ordered at the beginning.

35. But the intellect does not stop there. It notices that the *pleasant* or *painful* state of the human body corresponds to a certain disposition of parts and to an order in the shape, form, number, union and mutual action of these parts.[22] This *order*, to which the actually or habitually pleasant sensation corresponds, is considered as *perfection* in the human body. 'Perfection' is the state of the body co-existent with the pleasant feeling. Next, similar observations are made of all other animate, sensitive beings, and these are seen as perfect when all their parts and every thing in them maintains this *order*, which seems to produce for them the most pleasant existence. Finally the intellect sees that even external, inanimate objects are in varying ways suitable for serving its needs or those of other *sensitive* beings, provided the objects have a certain state, form and composition, which it accepts as their *perfection*.

36. In all these cases the word 'perfection' means an *order* intrinsic to things, corresponding to their most desired state. But how do we come to know this order? Strictly

from favouring nominalism, cuts the ground from under it. The *general value* determining numbers is precisely a *universal* concept. Hence a number is not simply a sign signifying nothing. On the contrary it is a sign or figure only when actually referring to a universal thought. Thus, it presupposes universals without explaining them.

[22] We perceive this order mainly with the extra-subjective mode of feeling. The relationship between feeling and perfection is the same as that between the subjective and extra-subjective modes of feeling. Unfortunately the very important difference between these two modes of feeling has not been grasped by many who have studied my philosophy. But my teaching cannot be understood without it.

speaking, *order* does not exist to itself or relative to feeling, because pleasant or painful feeling is a simple fact, no matter how mysteriously produced and irrelevant to the number of elements producing it. Order exists only to the understanding, although it is something more than the act of the understanding intuiting it. What I said earlier about *feeling* and the *matter* of feeling can also be said here: one cannot exist without the other; they are correlatives, and although different, have a simultaneous existence in the mental concept.

When we first form our concepts, therefore, the intrinsic *order* we give to the perfection of beings is deduced from their capacity to produce a constant, pleasant feeling for themselves or for us or any other thing in such a way that this capacity is the foundation, beginning and rule of that order. Later, however, we form more *special* concepts about the perfections in things because of the difficulty we have of returning to the first principle every time we want to measure the perfections. Hence, we form the concept of the intrinsic order of each thing, taking this order as a type or proximate criterion for judging its degrees of goodness. In other words, we often take the order as the essence and species of the thing.[23]

Once we have formed this species or essence, which presupposes an order beginning with action or the effect of action on our sensitivity, our understanding pays no further attention to the relationship with sensitive beings but concen-

[23] The following observation will help to demonstrate how we initially form this model of the intrinsic order of things from the connection they have with our pleasant sensations. Any natural being subject to the law of development passes through successive states, in each of which it is perfect because it necessarily is what it is. If, from all these possible states, we choose that in which the being has reached its final perfection, our choice is guided, as I have said, by our needs and pleasure; we say a being is perfect when it has reached the state of being most useful to us. For instance, it is the mature fruit, not the blossom which we consider as the final and perfect state of a fruit tree. But if we have no use for the fruit, we consider the blossom as the ultimate, perfect state. 'Flowering plants', as we call them, are a good example: the very name shows that we place their essence in producing flowers, not in producing seeds, because flowers give us a pleasant scent, while seeds give no pleasant sensations. This question merits further investigation, and those interested will be able to pursue it for themselves.

trates on enjoying the order as something beautiful and good in itself. It does not consider the purpose of the order but the energy that makes the order exist, that preserves, increases and develops the order until the complete essence is realised. This way of considering being concerns the intrinsic mode and order of being, in which the understanding grows accustomed to recognising a good.[24] Common sense is aware of this truth when it believes that the intelligence approves as good what belongs to the nature of a thing and harmonises with the nature's principle of existence. Clearly, anything opposing that principle is rejected as an evil, the sight of which causes a real disturbance in the being contemplating it. In short, everything tending to destroy a nature is considered opposed to it and harmful and evil. Reason disapproves of this opposition caused by disharmony and disorder because it is aware that something in a being is contradicting the being's essence. The essence therefore becomes the *rule* of the being's good and evil: anything required for the development and completion of the essence, far from destroying it, is *good*. Anything hostile and preventing its full development, is *evil*. Although in the beginning the essence had a relationship with sensitivity, that relationship is now forgotten.

37. This explanation of good and evil seems beyond doubt and is well within the grasp of the educated. In fact it does not exceed the level of reflection most human beings use for analysing or understanding their own ideas. We have said:

1. There are real beings, each of which can be found in a series of different states;

2. Human intelligence, using the relationship with

---

[24] There is a wonderful and very close harmony between the *order of being* considered in itself and the *order of being* relative to sensibility. An important but difficult investigation into this relationship needs to be made in *agathology*. The final result of such an investigation would be the inseparability of being and wisdom, the one unable to be thought without the other. I can only indicate it here. However I must point out that because our understanding is accustomed to positing the *perfection* of things in the order of being, it sometimes creates arbitrary, hypothetical beings and orders, which of course can only offer arbitrary and hypothetical perfection. Such creations of the human mind do not weaken the teaching we affirm, namely, that good is always referred to some faculty of feeling and desire.

sensitivity, chooses one of these states as perfect, and the type of perfection;

3. In this state as type, the intellect sees an order in which it finds good;

4. The order begins with existence and essence, to which are added the other elements, thus placing the thing in a state of perfection.

38. All the constitutives of a nature, therefore, have a single end (a perfect, typical state) to which all its forces unfailingly tend. This is the complete essence of the nature.[25] This simple end, by reason of its nature alone, is either in contradiction or harmony with certain modifications the thing receives. But our thought can penetrate more deeply and fix itself on the essential, necessary order of *being*. This order, which is intrinsic to *being*, excludes and admits certain things in natures, according to an intrinsic necessity, deduced and contemplated intuitively in the first fact, that is, in *being*, the primitive object of all thought. Every essence in fact is simply being, but more determined, limited, and actual than being as such. These determinations, limitations and acts have their origin and sole reason (and therefore their necessity) in being itself, which is determined, limited and actuated in those modes and not otherwise.

Having made these observations, we can finally give a definition of good sufficiently determined for our purposes.

39. Perfections or endowments of things are synonyms for 'good'. We think of them as causes of a pleasant feeling but we are able to contemplate them, independently of their effect, as something real, objective and active. *Good* therefore is more general than *sensations* and, although their cause and relative to them, precedes them. Things possess their perfections and what is good in the same way as they possess being. Thus, things with only a material existence, for example those lacking feeling, also have perfections relative to the beings perceiving them.

These endowments, and all that is good in a thing, are everything that harmonises with the thing's perfect existence, everything that tends to give the thing its fullness of being, whilst its (abstract) essence is, as it were, its theme, every-

---

[25] For *complete essence*, see *The Origin of Thought*, 646 ss.

thing to which the forces of the thing are directed as term of their movement. The name 'evil', on the other hand, is given to everything opposed to the thing, everything that *negates* it, stripping it of what necessarily belongs to it and of what it strives to possess with its interior activity.

40. *Abstract essence* is the principle of order; *complete essence* is its end. Between these two there is a gradation of perfection and good. The typical and *complete essence* is deduced from the relationship of the thing with feeling. But this relationship, and consequent order, exists for an intellective being by means of the intellect only, and provides therefore the notion of good. The consequences we can draw from this notion of good and evil are, first, that gradations of what is good can be present in every thing, beginning from its first, imperfect existence and continuing till its last development and completion. Secondly, anything that has been added to the thing to render it complete is only an act of its being, a level of its existence. A fitting conclusion for us, therefore, is the opinion of the ancient world that *everything is good in so far as it is, and evil in so far as it is not*.

41. *Good* then is identical with *being* and is being. If being is realised, actuated and developed, it has an intrinsic, necessary order of actuation and development whose explanation is found only in itself. This order is such that one thing requires or excludes another, just as the roots of a tree require the trunk, the branches and finally the fruit if the tree is to be complete. When the intrinsic order of a thing's actuation and development requires some addition, the addition is good; when it excludes something, what is excluded is evil. *Sensitiveness* is concerned with good but only because feeling itself belongs to being, of which it is an act. The nature of being requires a relationship between *matter* and *sensitiveness* for good to exist. The same is true for the understanding, which is also an act of being.

Being and *good* therefore are the same. 'Good' is 'being considered in its order', and the order, when known, is enjoyed by the intelligence. 'Good' is 'being as felt, in relationship with the intelligence', in so far as the intelligence sees both what every nature requires and that to which it tends with its forces in the way described.

42. I conclude with a quotation from the *Summa* of St. Thomas, who is generally considered the best witness to christian tradition: 'Good and being are really the same but differ conceptually. The concept of good comprises the thing as desirable. It is clear that everything is desirable in so far as it is perfect because all things desire their own perfection. But anything is perfect, in so far as it has the act of being. Hence a thing is good in so far as it is a being, because being is the actuality of everything.'[26]

Article 2.
The nature of evil

43. All that has been said in the previous article also applies to the notion of evil, but it will help understanding if I add another observation.

We have seen that in all the possible constitutives of any being there is an order by which these constitutives are determined and distinguished from all others. There is a class of qualities and conditions that harmonise with every nature, and a class foreign or opposed to the nature. These possible constitutives or entities are necessary in different ways to the being and are considered its good according to its needs. Now, if both good and evil imply a relationship of harmony or disharmony with the principle of the being they effect, that is, with its essence, then to exist, the good and evil presuppose the subject of which they are predicated. I say both good and evil because, while we cannot doubt that good requires being, indeed is being itself, we could think that evil, as a negation or absence, does not presuppose being.

44. We have to remember that, although everything is good in so far as it is and has being, we cannot say that a total negation of being is an evil. A total negation leaves only nothingness. Nothingness is nothing, which is neither evil nor good. I have said that evil involves a relationship with a being, with the subject possessing it. Evil is a negation, not of the whole being, but of some part which is absent and needed by the being. We thus recognise that the absence is repugnant to the principle of the being. A human body, for example,

[26] *S.T.* I, q. 5, art. 1.

missing an arm or leg, would suffer an evil because it lacked an integral part required by the intrinsic order of the essence of a human being. The absence indicates to our intelligence an imperfection in that nature, something contrary to its intrinsic, immutable order. For this reason the word 'privation' rather than 'negation' was used to mean evil. 'Negation' is too general and vague, expressing the removal not only of the parts but of the whole. 'Privation' expresses the removal of the parts but not of the whole being; it includes the idea of a being deprived of something, but not absolutely annihilated.

Article 3.
The idea of being is the notion with which we make judgments about good in general

45. *Being* and *good* are the same thing; every nature is good in so far as it is and evil in so far as it lacks any part of being belonging to it. An analysis of what is commonly understood by the word 'good' shows that the being of every nature has an intrinsic order determining the necessity of certain parts and qualities, which become what is good and perfect for the nature. Consequently, we know the good or value or grade of perfection of any nature when we know its being and the many grades it has of the existence proper to it, that is, when we know the order possessed by its being and expressed in its essence. The order is understood in the idea, and the more perfect the idea the better understood is the order. We need to know how much of the order of being has been realised, developed and completed or how much is missing and needed for its completion. Knowledge therefore of a thing's being or its mode or order of being is also knowledge of its goodness. Thus, the notion of being alone is sufficient for me to measure and determine both the grades of real existence of a thing and its perfection, because both are found together in the same thing.

If *being* and *good* are the same, knowledge of being must also be knowledge of good,[27] because being has only to be

[27] Because the idea of good is nothing more than the idea of being, we can understand the truth of Plato's statement, 'all knowledge is founded on the idea of good.'

considered in its intrinsic order for it to be called 'good'. Therefore the idea of being is the notion, rule and principle with which I measure and identify the good of all the natures I perceive and know.

3

THE IDEA OF BEING
AS THE PRINCIPLE OF EUDAIMONOLOGY

Article 1.
Definition of eudaimonology

46. Eudaimonology teaches the way to one's own happiness and differs from ethics, although the two are easily confused or at least not sufficiently separated. One modern school has in fact made the confusion systematic to the detriment of ethics and human dignity. But only ethics draws human nature away from self, and leads us to forget our own interest in the search for what is just and upright.

Nevertheless, we have to acknowledge that Kant and his school have liberated ethics from the stimulus of happiness. Unfortunately, however, they concentrated their attention on finding a final[28] stimulus to moral good, and did not succeed in establishing the true nature of morality itself. Lacking the necessary characteristics to be moral, their stimulus was unreasonable and unjustified, and imposed itself upon human nature cruelly and fatalistically. It prevented the progress which would have resulted in a scientific view of ethics and the discovery of a firm foundation for moral science.

Article 2.
The idea of being is the principle of eudaimonology

47. We have seen that the idea of being is the principle by

---

[28] Many writers in Germany have at times been inadvertently subject to this error. They have begun their moral works by establishing two stimuli, happiness and rectitude, as a basic fact of human existence. But this is not sufficient for morality, which must not derive from a *stimulus* or an instinct. If morality were an instinct, it would not be obligatory, because obligation is something opposed to instinct; it directs all instincts, requiring human beings to follow its direction. If morality were only a stimulus, it would not be based on reason. *Reasonableness* is the characteristic of morality, and it is neither a stimulus nor an instinct. We must therefore look for the principle of the moral law in *reason*, not in a primitive stimulus.

which we judge good in general, and consequently the principle enabling us to know what is good or evil, fitting or unfitting, for us. It is, therefore, the supreme principle of the science of our own happiness and as such the rule according to which we measure our own good and degrees of happiness.

It is clear, however, that as a principle the idea of being is common to many branches of knowledge; it is not confined to eudaimonology in which only my own subjective good, not all good, is the object of reference. In a word, the idea of being, as the idea of good in general, is too extensive to be the proper, exclusive principle of eudaimonology. Knowledge of happiness has as its object the more restricted notion of human, subjective good. It will be helpful if we outline the subjective good proper to human beings so as to avoid confusing it with what is good in itself.

Article 3.
Subjective good

48. *Subjective* good is good considered relatively to a subject enjoying it. Good in itself, absolute good, is never considered relatively to any subject whatsoever.

49. If something good in itself is to be good for a certain subject there must be some kind of harmony between the good and the subject, or rather between the subject and what is good. The nature of the subject has to be such that it can fittingly adjust and adhere to that good, forming almost a single entity with it and thus enjoying it. But it happens very often that a subject is incapable of enjoyable union with things which, although good in themselves, are either neutral or evil relative to itself. This explains why a feelable good means nothing to natures which, lacking feeling, cannot condition themselves to the enjoyment of feelable good. In the same way, virtue, wisdom and other supra-sensible good is meaningless relative to animals. Such good can be perceived and enjoyed only with the intellect and reason that animals lack. Wisdom and virtue are the highest good for beings which possess intellect and will, for whom alone, as we shall see, absolute good exists.

Each thing is good in itself, but not good for any subject whatsoever. Certain things do not even exist for some subjects; others are bad and harmful for some subjects, but good for others. Normally, however, we look upon good subjectively and relatively to ourselves, rather than objectively and in itself. As a result we often lose sight completely of good in its objective concept, which we tend to deny totally; and we go on to characterise as a paradox (despising perhaps those who hold it) any statement affirming all things as good, or declaring good to be any thing that is in so far as it is. Realising that not all beings are good for us, or good for people in general, we conclude that not all beings are good. This would be correct if it were applied to subjective or relative good alone; it is false when applied to good in general.

Many people can neither rise above relative good nor step outside themselves, although careful consideration would show them that there is no being or perfection of being which is not good for some subject, or not good for itself. It would then be easy for them to see that every being contains the necessary conditions for good, which are simply that it be good towards itself, complete and tending with the forces proper to its nature towards its own preservation and perfection.[29]

Hence the ancient definition of good as that which all things desire (*quod omnia appetunt*), where *desire* is understood in its broadest sense as any tendency whatsoever of the forces proper to a nature. As I said, every being shows in this sense that it desires itself, that is, possesses an energy through which it exists, remains in existence, and reaches perfection. The definition shows that good considered in its very own concept is found to consist in the appetite or tendency that

---

[29] Inanimate beings resist their destruction with the forces they possess, that is, the forces with which they subsist. This is so intrinsic and necessary to each nature that simply declaring a nature is, means that it continually strives to maintain its existence, while ceaselessly struggling against its annihilation. However, we have said that this necessary characteristic, which gives all things the notion of good in themselves, is imperfect in inanimate natures in exactly the same measure as their being, which they neither feel nor know they possess. They are good, therefore, in a relative sense rather than in a proper sense.

things have towards themselves, not towards being desired, loved or attracted by other things. 'Being desired' only shows that one thing is good for another, not that it is a good to itself; it expresses the concept of relative good, not of good as such.

50. Taken simply and purely, the concept of good as a basis for reason is common to all beings and all degrees of beings; each being is aptly said to be good in so far as it is. The notion of good in itself is not to be confused therefore with the notion of relative good. It is one thing for a being to be good for itself, and thus good in itself, and another for it to be good for some other being. Being good for itself is what constitutes the simple notion of good; being good for some other being constitutes the notion of relative good. If a thing is good for something other than itself we can conclude only that it possesses a relationship of goodness, and consequently is good in that particular respect without being good in its entirety, in its being. We cannot conclude simply that it is good. It is good in the effect it produces in something different from itself, but if that were its totality of good it could not be called true, actual good in itself. At most it would be *potentially* good, or have the power to *do* some good.

Article 4.
The principle underlying eudaimonology

51. The object of eudaimonology is human happiness, a subjective good we have already described. But knowledge of subjective good in general is not sufficient for understanding the notion that serves as the proper principle of the branch of science we are studying.

Human happiness, as a subjective good proper to intelligent beings, is a specific subjective good whose notion forms the special principle of eudaimonology.

The aim of this book is to explain the principles of ethics, not those of eudaimonology, although it has been necessary to mention the latter in order to avoid the modern danger of confusing it with the former. But *happiness* does have a very close connection with *justice*, and it will be helpful, and perhaps necessary, to add a few words about the notion of happiness as the supreme and perfect good of mankind.

Article 5.
The good of existence and the good of perfection

52. When we think of any subject whatsoever we first mentally conceive its existence and then its perfection. In every subject there is something without which the subject cannot exist. This is usually called its substance or specific essence.[30] There is also something without which the subject can exist, but only imperfectly. These are its accidental perfections. When these *accidental perfections* are added to its *specific essence*, the subject reaches fulfilment because these perfections as developments of its act of being are consequently acquired degrees of being.

53. Being, however, is divided into *substantial* and *accidental*, and these divisions have to be predicated of good also. It is a fundamental truth, as we have seen, that being and good are distinguished from one another only because viewed in different ways.

It is impossible for a subject to desire or tend towards existence before it possesses existence. Nothing can act before it begins to exist. But when a subject has already begun to exist, it can demonstrate its tendency to develop and perfect itself, and to preserve itself if its existence is attacked. This twofold tendency towards its *preservation* and *perfect development* is the double good — existential good and perfect good — that we have distinguished in the title of this article.

54. But the final term towards which all the forces of any subject whatsoever tend and are ceaselessly directed is its perfect development. It is this ultimate term of desire (or more universally, of the tendencies in every nature) which is commonly called 'good', as St. Thomas observes: 'Good indicates something relative to perfection, which is the object of desire. Consequently good has in itself some concept of finality' (that is, it is the final term of 'desire', or the final

[30] Cf. my teaching on *essence* in *The Origin of Thought*, 646 ss.

completion of the thing). 'Hence, what we normally call "good" simply and purely is that which is finally perfect. But if something has not reached the final perfection of which it is capable, although it does possess the good of existence, we call it perfect or good in a restricted sense; as *good*, it is such under some particular aspect. Relative to its first or substantial being, therefore, the thing is called simply *being*, and is *good* only in so far as it is; relative to its final act of being, that is, its perfection, the thing is *good* simply, and *being* relatively (in so far as it is good).'[31]

This distinction between the good of existence and the good of perfection is equally applicable to the evils of *destruction* and *deterioration*.

Article 6.
The evil of deterioration and the evil of destruction

55. Nothingness, as we have seen, is not evil; nevertheless, we can distinguish between the evil of destruction and that of deterioration. We mentally conceive these two species of evil in the following way.

56. Whenever a cause of any kind acts in a subject in such a way as to lessen the subject's degree of being, that cause is harmful to the subject. But we have to distinguish the time in which the cause acts from the time in which it has already produced its effect. While the cause acts, the subject suffers. The subject experiences the action of the cause and reacts with the forces available to it in order to protect itself. This struggle is already an evil, provoking pain in the subject because its perfection, or even its existence, is lessened.

57. If the effect has been to destroy and annihilate the subject, we have to say that no evil remains because there is

---

[31] *Bonum dicit rationem perfecti, quod est appetibile; et per consequens dicit rationem ultimi. Unde id, quod est ultimo perfectum dicitur bonum simpliciter: quod autem non habet ultimam perfectionem quam debet habere, quamvis habeat aliquam perfectionem inquantum est actu, non tamen dicitur perfectum simpliciter, nec bonum simpliciter, sed secundum quid. Sic ergo secundum primum esse, quod est substantiale, dicitur aliquid* ENS *simpliciter, et* BONUM *secundum quid, id est, inquantum* ENS: *secundum vero ultimum actum dicitur aliquid* ENS *secundum quid, et* BONUM *simpliciter.* S.T. I, q. 5, art. 1, ad 1.

no longer any subject capable of experiencing good or evil. Nevertheless, while the action tending to destroy the subject was taking place, the subject was suffering an actual evil which continued to increase until the subject was finally eliminated. It is the experience of this continual violence of gradual deterioration through to annihilation that is called *the evil of destruction*. If the effect of the cause's action resulted only in a lessening of the perfection of the subject, but not its total destruction, the evil remains after the cessation of action because the subject, the seat of the evil, is still in existence.

It is clear, therefore, that the evil of destruction exists only as long as destruction is not complete. But with the destruction of the subject, no evil is left. The evil of deterioration, however, has two modes, one in the transitory *act* in which it is produced, and the other in a *state* of habitual and permanent evil after it has been produced.

Article 7.
Absolute good

58. To avoid all ambiguity we have to distinguish the *absolute notion* of good from *absolute good*.

Being and good do not differ in reality. Everything which has some degree of existence is also good to that degree.

The being which things possess, making them good in themselves, enables us to affirm that they fall within the absolute notion of good. This *absolute notion* is in contradistinction to the *relative notion* of good whereby one thing is considered good relatively to another, not to itself. If absolute good is understood therefore as that which falls within the *absolute notion* of good, it can be said that everything possesses its own absolute good. Here, absolute good is distinguished from relative good which is founded on the relative notion of good, that is, on something considered as the cause of good in others.

59. However, the two statements, 'Every subject has an absolute good in itself' and 'Every subject falls within the absolute notion of good', may be considered at a deeper level where the latter is altogether correct, and the former less so.

This depends upon the difference between *good* and the *notion of good*, between real good itself and the idea or concept of good.

60. The notion of good does not involve the degrees of good because this notion is universal and common to any degree of good however small it may be. The notion is realised and verified in the slightest as well as the greatest good. But real, subsistent good is found in various degrees. In this sense the notion of good is absolute and perfect in every degree of good although good itself cannot be absolute and perfect unless it is present in its highest and final degree. In a word, there is an absolute and a relative notion of good.

The absolute notion of good consists in that towards which the forces of each being tend; the relative notion consists in the aptitude a being has for causing good for others. Strictly speaking, therefore, each thing in so far as it is good to itself lies within the absolute notion of good; but we cannot say that each thing is an absolute good.[32]

Absolute good is only that which has all good in itself, just

---

[32] The difference between *good* and the *idea* or *notion of good* corresponds to the difference between *being* and the *idea of being*. The *idea of being* is the same as *possible being* or, as I commonly call it, *initial being*. This initial or possible being, this idea of being (all these terms signify the same) is the *means* by which the human spirit knows things — as I have shown in *The Origin of Thought* [473-557]. However, in order to perceive beings as *subsistent* and not simply *possible*, human beings need *feeling*, which is the power of perceiving the real subsistence of things. But the perception of the subsistence of things in itself is not *knowledge*. To become *knowledge*, it must be joined to thought or the intuition of *possibility*, which is simply the universal notion of being itself. Thus I showed that the *knowledge* of a thing consists 'in the vision formed by the spirit of the relationship between the thing's subsistence and its possibility'. I placed the specific characteristic of *human knowledge* in this vision. For this reason, *possible being*, the noble medium of human knowledge, *specifies* human nature, forming the specific characteristic which distinguishes this nature from all others. In the same way, therefore, that *being in potency* (principle of knowledge) differs fundamentally from *beings in act* (objects of knowledge), the *notion of good* or good in potency differs fundamentally from *good* in act. The same difference is found in everything we know, for example, between the notion of beauty and beauty itself, between the notion of greatness and greatness itself, between the notion of body and the body itself, between the notion of animal and the animal itself, etc.

as absolute being is only that which has all being in itself. And in saying this, we really mean not that which has all being in itself, but that which is all being. Complete being is complete good.

61. The nature of our intelligence is formed by being, but only by initial, potential being. If we were to behold this being in its fullness, in its act, in the term of its act, we would see absolute being. This follows necessarily from our premises. If it is true that good is being and that we see being naturally but imperfectly, it must also be true that if this being were to reveal itself more perfectly to our minds, already created by its imperfect presence, we would see good itself, essential good, and therefore entire, absolute good. Because nothing is lacking to this being, and hence to this good, it must be absolute.

Moreover, because nothing is, except through being, being is at the origin of all things as the original act of every nature. As such it is also the source of all that is good and, as St. Augustine says, 'It is the good of every good.' This explains why perfect being is not only the highest good in itself and for itself, but the highest good relative to everything else. And this complete, absolute being, which is also the highest and absolute good, is called God.

Article 8.
Happiness

62. Having explained what we mean by absolute good, we can now form an idea of the happiness to which human beings tend. This notion is the object of *eudaimonology*, which must be distinguished from *ethics*. To confuse the two branches of knowledge would lead to the irreparable destruction of ethics.

What is good for human beings? Their good relative to *existence* is *human* existence, that is, human nature.

The good upon which human *perfection* depends is determined by the two substances, corporeal and spiritual, which compose our human nature and subsist in a single subject ('myself'), the 'human being'. We must therefore discover the good proper to each of the two substances, and to the human being as a whole.

In so far as human beings are animal subjects furnished with bodily sense, they are capable of adapting for themselves, and enjoying, only particular, corporeal good.

63. As intellective subjects, however, they perceive all species of good, and enjoy all the good they have perceived. The human[33] intellect can even attain to absolute good, which alone therefore can satisfy it entirely and fully.[34] Absolute good is the highest good of intelligences, and when enjoyed provides *bliss* or happiness, terms never used of the blind, momentary movements of animal life or of any perfection connected with non-sensitive things. It is indeed reasonable to reserve such words as *bliss* and *happiness* to describe the full, perpetual, final and, in some ways, infinite enjoyment that contrasts so vividly with limited, instantaneous pleasure.[35]

Outside the highest good there is nothing capable of filling the human heart and rendering it fully satisfied and content.

[33] The intellect is considered as a feeling (and therefore called *intellective feeling*) when its act is observed solely within the understanding subject. If we analyse the thought of any object whatever, the thought is present under two aspects: as an experience affecting my spirit and caused by the object I am thinking; as an act of the subject terminating in the object. As an experience, I call the thought a *sensation*; as an act of the subject I call it *knowledge*. The experience is something affecting the subject and totally in the subject, in which it is terminated and consumed. It is therefore an interior sensation, an act of intellectual feeling. The affection or thought, however, considered as a means of knowing the object and as an act of the spirit allowing the spirit to posit both itself and something *different* from itself, is an act of the *cognitive faculty*. In other words, to feel is to unite and make one with oneself. It presupposes various states of a subject, which are identified through the identity of the subject; to know presupposes an absolute difference between the knowing subject and what is known.

[34] In the present life this greatest good is an object of *faith* and therefore of christian hope; it is not seen but believed. Reasoning itself, however, in its present state of development, leads us to know that the final term of intelligence can only be the absolute being, God.

[35] *Sensists* err because they inevitably confuse *happiness* with *pleasure*, measuring the amount of happiness by the amount of pleasure. Happiness is certainly an enjoyment but not any enjoyment — it is the enjoyment of the greatest good. And the difference between enjoying the greatest good and enjoying any other good is not one of degree but of species; it is an infinite difference with no middle term uniting the two extremes. [. . .]

The intimate nature of every intellective being is formed, as we have said so often, by the idea of universal being which enables us to know every being and every good. When, therefore, the will of an intelligent being has as its end a good less than the absolute good, it can always go further without having to limit its desires. The will can want as much as the intellect knows. But the intellect can know ever greater good until it arrives at the complete, highest good that is good itself, being itself, the absolute. It can go no further because this is the final, ultimate good. Only here can and must the will be at rest because its desire cannot be satisfied until it reaches and embraces essential good. In this good alone lies true bliss for the intellective nature, and the supreme dignity and beauty which distances it immeasurably from other natures. Its capacity for intimate union with the absolute good makes it one with this good. Herein lies the final excellence of all creation. Other perfections of created nature can be considered as means, but the bliss we have spoken of must be thought and considered as an end.

64. So far we have examined the good of perfection of the two substances forming the mixed subject we call 'a human being.' But what is the relationship between the two substances, which forms the good of the entire human being?

The principal relationship between the two elements forming human beings depends upon the dignity of the intellective over the animal element, and upon the dignity of the good of the intellective element over the good of the animal element. We are dealing with a relationship between end and means. If the sole, absolute good is the end, everything else is a means to be ordered and subjected to absolute good. It is true that in this life we do not know the absolute good positively and entirely, and cannot therefore behold the connection, revealed through intimate meditation, by which all good, including corporeal good, has its source in the supreme Being who uses it as a way of communicating himself. Nevertheless, we see that this must be the case, and realise that there can be no intrinsic opposition and contradiction between corporeal good and the essential good, just as there can be no opposition between a spring of water and the stream flowing from it. In the same way, human beings, if they possess essential, intellective good, cannot lack any happiness of which their corporeal element is capable although this happiness will be granted in such a way as not to impose limits or impediments to the satisfaction of their intellective element. The bodily part of the human being will share the joy of the intellective source.

65. A final observation to this article. In our present existence, the animal good of human nature shares in human dignity because in our present existence it is ordered to intellectual good. The human subject is undivided: I experience corporeal sensations, and I reason about them. If anyone harms my body, therefore, he harms ME. And because I possess the dignity proper to an intellective being, he injures the intellective principle that constitutes my personality. All good belonging to an intelligent subject is immediately or mediately an object appertaining to intelligence, the principal element characterising and specifying such a subject.

Article 9.
The dignity of the intelligent subject

66. The dignity of the intelligent subject arises, as I have observed, from the dignity of the idea of being, the source of the subject's understanding. Being, the first object of knowledge and the source of all our other knowledge, is universal, unlimited and infinite, and alone renders the mind capable of knowing all the *genera* and *species* of good, and enjoying such knowledge. The nature of this knowledge and enjoyment is characterised by a truly supreme and infinite dignity. It enables the intelligent subject to forget self by considering things as they are in themselves; to look at things impartially and justly; and in so doing, to render homage to being itself, without thought of self, in all the degrees in which it knows being.

The objectivity found in intellective contemplation is in a certain sense infinite, as I said, because it has no limits. It is capable of making known all things, even infinite things, as they are and whatever they are. And *infinity* is the fundamental principle of *dignity*. Wherever we are engaged with something infinite, we are dealing with something so great and awesome that finite things give way before it. In its presence, they experience a sublime sense of their own nothingness in thinking of this being which, transcending them, calls forth unlimited reverence for its own veiled, obscure grandeur. The *primary* dignity of the intelligent subject, therefore, lies in the contemplation of truth.

67. *Secondly*, the vision in which the intelligent subject sees universal being is that in which it would see the absolute, subsistent being if it were to reveal itself in its act of subsistence rather than as an idea. The intelligence, furnished with its *intellective sense*, is constituted to perceive absolute being and absolute good, and so to perceive once more the infinite. Only in this perception can its forces be fully consumed. This direction towards absolute, infinite being is the *second* cause of the dignity possessed by the intellective being. There is no greater good to which it could be related.

Finally, the perception of absolute being implies union with and possession of absolute being, the source of bliss and of infinite enjoyment. The capacity for enjoying this bliss is the *third* and last cause of dignity in human beings and every other intelligent nature.

68. This happiness, towards which human nature tends unceasingly, and the means for attaining it, are the subject of *eudaimonology*.

We can now return to *ethics* and try to penetrate its nature at a deeper level.

4

THE IDEA OF BEING AS THE PRINCIPLE OF ETHICS

Article 1.
Summary

69. In the last chapter I digressed from my subject in order to indicate the nature of the branch of science dealing with human subjective good, and showed how it is essentially different from ethics. It will help us now if we first sum up what has been said before returning to the principles which are our first concern. We concluded that:

1, the idea of being is the supreme rule of all the judgments made by the human mind;

2, the idea of being is consequently the supreme rule of moral judgments and as such the first and most universal of all laws;

3, this law can be expressed in the dictate: 'Follow the light of reason', the most all-embracing of the declarations found in ethics;

4, because the idea of being is the rule of all judgments, including moral judgments, it is a principle common to many branches of knowledge;

5, because *being* and *good* are the same thing, the notion of being is also the notion of good and in a special way the principle of all branches of knowledge concerned with what is good;

6, finally, it is not sufficient to indicate a common principle of science without assigning to every branch of knowledge its own *proper* principle. And this, in the case of *eudaimonology*, is the notion of human subjective good, that is, happiness.

70. In the present chapter, we shall begin to investigate the principle proper to ethics. It is clear that if we succeed in discovering and describing such a principle, we shall also be able to throw light on the first, supreme moral law, which consists in the most sublime application of being. We shall see that this uniquely important use of the light of reason can be

summed up in a single word, and we shall have answered the question we set ourselves: how can being be used in a practical way to enable us to differentiate what is just from what is unjust, and what is right from what is wrong?

Article 2.
Objective good

71. If we are to understand how the notion of being can serve as moral law, we have to clarify our notion of the essence of morality and moral good.

72. Moral good is certainly good of some kind. This is sufficient for us to understand that judgments about it require first of all the notion of good in general. We cannot know what a particular good is unless we first know what good is. In our definition of moral good, therefore, we are simply restricting the universal notion of good so that it becomes the notion proper to ethics and the special kind of good with which ethics is concerned. But if we succeed in determining and restricting the notion of good with the characteristics which render it moral, we shall have taken certain steps in acknowledging it as the principle proper to ethics. We shall have shown how the idea of being gradually approaches, as it were, moral good and evil, while awakening and enlightening us so that we may know, distinguish and measure them. The universality of the first principles prevents their being applied immediately without the mediation of other restricted principles descending from them and forming a link between the universal principles on the one hand and particulars on the other. What is *moral good*, therefore?

73. To clarify the notion we must first say something about objective good, that is, every good in so far as it is perceived objectively or becomes an object of knowledge. As we have seen, the absolute notion of good consists in that which befits the intrinsic order of being in every nature and to which all the forces of a given nature tend. The relative notion of good, on the other hand, consists in something desirable to another and as such the term and aim of the forces natural to this other nature, which move towards and tend to unite possessively with what is desirable. These notions provide us with

knowledge of two kinds of good, the good of things in themselves, and the good of things relative to other things. Both kinds of good become *objects* of our intelligence, and thus *objective*.

74. Our act of understanding is of itself universal. That is, our faculty of knowledge, instead of knowing good itself, knows how to conceive mentally the reason or concept of good. Consequently we can know, through possession of such a faculty, everything to which the notion of good extends — such an extension of knowledge demonstrates the universality itself of the intellectual act. Because our understanding conceives every species of good, every good can be considered by us objectively.

The opposite is true of bodily feeling, which perceives good itself without conceiving the reason for what is good. Moreover, bodily feeling perceives and enjoys only the particular good it finds proportioned to itself.

75. The intellectual subject, therefore, in some way unites to himself and enjoys the good in every nature. It is true that knowledge alone cannot entail perfect possession and enjoyment of what is good because knowledge provides only the notion of good as a basis of reason, not the good itself. Nevertheless, a sublime, although imperfect, joy pervades the human being at the mental conception of even the abstract reason of good. This enables us to conclude that the intellectual spirit is possessed, even in this life, of a certain intellectual sense[36] with which it enjoys the essences and concepts of good. This sense, unlike corporeal sense, is not limited to a

---

[36] This *intellective feeling* was known to all the early thinkers and is found in ecclesiastical tradition. In his *Retractions* St. Augustine recalls having written in one of his books 'we must despise what sense perceives' when he should have written 'what bodily feeling perceives' because, as he says, *est sensus et mentis* [there is also feeling of the mind]. But he excuses himself at once by adding (and this will also serve as an explanation of those places where I might have used the word *sense* to mean what is simply corporeal): *Eorum more tunc loquebar, qui sensum non nisi corporis dicunt, et sensibilia non nisi corporalia. Itaque ubicumque sic locutus sum, parum est ambiguitas evitata, nisi apud eos quorum consuetudo est locutionis hujus* [At that time I spoke like those who use the word 'feeling' only for the body and 'feelable' only for bodily things. Consequently there is some ambiguity wherever I have spoken in this way, except for those who use the words with the above meaning]. bk. 1, chap. 1.

particular good, but expands to take in all the objects of the intelligence so that the satisfaction it achieves depends not on itself, but on things in themselves, that is, considered objectively. We shall understand this better after comparing this objective good with good considered subjectively.

Article 3.
The relationship between objective and subjective good

76. *Sense* and *intellect* comprise the two fundamental human faculties. They perceive things in different ways and thus provide the explanation of the distinction between *subjective* and *objective* good. Sense is the source of subjective good; the intellect of objective good.

77. In fact, every *feelable good* is *subjective*, that is, good to the subject uniting it to itself and feeling it. But good intuited by the mind as the object of thought, that is, *intelligible good*, is *objective* because it is considered as it is in itself, in the way in which it is, and not as belonging to the thinking subject. The good enjoyed by a particular subject, if it is indeed subjective good, cannot be other than feelable because only sense, whether corporeal or intellectual, can enjoy it. The opposite is true of the way in which the understanding sees good as *objective*. Here the intelligent subject comes to know a wider range of good things than those which affect him. He knows that many things are good, although they may not be good for him. But if he had no reasoning faculty, he would have no means of knowing any good which he did not experience through his senses. It would not exist for him.

78. Objective good, therefore, extends far beyond subjective good which, as subjective, is good proper to the subject. Objective good is any good whatsoever, whether proper to the subject contemplating it (and hence subjective) or not, provided it is contemplated as it is by the intelligence.

79. But there is another way of explaining the relationship between subjective and objective good. I have already shown that the human subject ('myself') is not only essentially sentient, but a substantial feeling.[37] Sensations are only

---

[37] *Certainty*, 1195 ss.

modifications of 'myself' — modifications of a substantial feeling which is partly unchangeable and partly changeable. The *identity* of this subjective feeling depends upon what is unchangeable; the *diversity* of the sensations it experiences depends upon what is changeable. The human subject always feels himself, or rather his mode of being. Feeling is inseparable from the subject; it begins and ends in the subject, with which it identifies itself. Hence *subjective good* has its origin in *sense*.

80. Intelligence is characterised in a totally different way. With intelligence, we conceive mentally and come to know *objectively*; the act of understanding begins in the subject, but terminates in an object conceived as independent of the subject conceiving it. In fact, the subject is excluded altogether because it never conceives itself, but only the term of its mental conception. Only intelligence therefore can conceive what is good in itself. It is clear that *objective good* depends for its origin on the understanding.

81. Nevertheless, although the act of understanding terminates outside the subject, the intellective subject obtains a unique enjoyment from the objects of its understanding considered in themselves. Everyone has experienced the joy that knowledge brings, and appreciates the truth expressed by Marcus Tullius: *Natura inest mentibus nostris insatiabilis quaedam cupiditas veri vivendi* ['Nature provides our minds with an insatiable longing to live the truth'].[38]

We have, therefore, a mental sense enabling us to savour all the objects we know. Through this sense, the *objective* good known by an intelligent being inevitably becomes *subjective* because of the enjoyment it engenders in the intelligent subject.[39]

Above all, we have to note the extraordinary purity of enjoyment engendered in us by a cause totally different from that which prompts the pleasure found in purely subjective good. The purely sensitive subject enjoys subjective good because this good terminates totally in the subject. The intellective subject enjoys objective good because by going outside

[38] *Tusculanae Disputationes*, bk. 1, chap. 19.
[39] The contrary is not true. Only in the case of absolute good does a subjective good act to make itself objective.

himself through the thought of objective good, he mentally expands his existence in other objects; he enjoys contemplating them impartially and fully in themselves, not simply in the particular relationship they have with himself; and finally he rejoices in his consciousness of justice towards these objects by his acknowledgement of what is good in them regardless of self. Justice, disinterestedness and reverence towards truth are contained essentially in the act of knowledge, and consummated by acceptance on the part of the will. The result is a sublime delight accompanying the intellective subject along the path of knowledge.

Article 4.
The relationship between objective and absolute good

82. A further step in clarifying the nature of *objective good* is taken by comparing objective with *absolute good*. We have seen that absolute good and absolute being are the same. We have also seen that in our present condition our mind, although it sees and uses being to know all that it knows, sees being only initially, in potency. Finally, we noted that if this potential being were to be realised in act, being as seen by the mind would pass from the ideal to the subsistent state and would, in this case, be absolute being. The mind would then see God. *Absolute being*, therefore, is essentially *objective being* and cannot be possessed by the human subject except through an act of intelligence. Nevertheless, we rightly affirm the existence of an intellective sense in so far as the intelligence attains absolute being as its proper good. Sense is the power that perceives subsistent things, in contradistinction to the intellect as the faculty of knowledge that intuits possible things.

Article 5.
Objective good is the source of moral good,
subjective good the source of good as well-being

83. But what is *moral good*? Is it good considered subjectively or objectively?

Moral good is undoubtedly an objective, not a subjective good. A subject searching only for his own satisfaction does nothing moral. He obeys the instinct[40] for pleasure or happiness, but pays no attention to other beings which have the same or greater rights than himself. As long as he thinks only of himself he remains at the level of self-love, egotistically rejecting the good he knows but cannot possess. In a word, this subject is formed by sense whose nature and laws become part of himself.

84. Intelligence, however, is not limited to subjective good, as we have seen. It conceives every good impartially, considering each good in itself, measuring its degree of goodness disinterestedly. This is possible because intelligence possesses the idea of being, which is the measure of the various degrees of existence and hence of the various grades of good. It considers being and good objectively, and in doing so shows the disinterestedness which forms a natural exercise of justice capable of ennobling the act of intelligence. Moral good, therefore, can be found only in objective good because only in the act of reason can the principle of justice, which gives to each his own (the great formula of moral legislation), be found.

85. Thus we find ourselves brought back to the first moral law which we expressed at the beginning of this work, 'Act according to the light of reason.' What has been said confirms and clarifies this law, and clearly demonstrates the error of those who want to base ethics on pleasure or self-interest, however enlightened. Ethics is concerned with *duty* and obligation towards an object considered in itself by the intelligence, not with *pleasure* and self-interest which in the last analysis always regard the subject.

86. Helvetius in France, Bentham in England and Gioja and Romagnosi° in Italy confused the subject with the object, and thus annihilated morality, reducing it to the art of looking after one's own self-interest. But, as we have seen, when the subject is carefully distinguished from the object we

---

[40] Two active faculties correspond to the two passive faculties of *feeling* and *intelligence* that we have distinguished in the human being. *Instinct* corresponds to feeling, *will* to intelligence. The instinct inclines to pleasure and *happiness*, while the will is the principle of *morality*.

are presented with two opposite principles of two opposite, non-identifiable branches of knowledge. Ethics begins with the object as its principle, and deals with morality; eudaimonology has the subject as its foundation, and deals with happiness. It would seem that even classical philosophy was not sufficiently clear about this distinction, and amalgamated the two branches of knowledge into one practical science containing indiscriminately whatever could be said about either. However, there are many places in which the authors show they were not unaware of the disparity and opposition between morality and utility.

87. The morally good act, therefore, has objective good as its term, that is, good in so far as it is contemplated and judged as good by the intelligence. On this basis, a being is not morally good in so far as its instinct moves and stimulates it towards its own pleasure and good. In such a case it does not tend towards good because it is good, but because it is its own good. It loves itself, not good as such. This is restrictive love, excluding what is good because it is not the subject's own, and hence terminating in injustice, in non-love, in a kind of depravity. The aim of the morally good subject, who follows lovingly the light of his reason, is more elevated. He loves good for its own sake, in its proper nature as good, as intelligence shows it to him. Hence he loves good *wherever* it appears to him; he loves *every* good, and by contemplating good attains willingly the pure, noble joy that naturally results in a good, intelligent subject from good as known. He disregards himself because his guide, the understanding, prescinds of its nature from the subject. The understanding is outside the subject; it is independent, impersonal, absolute; it is truth itself, impartiality itself. It loves all objects, all beings. And because intelligence is formed by the vision of universal being, morality is formed by *universal love* — the love of all beings, of every good — love which extends as far as knowledge, infinitely.

88. 'Follow the light of reason' is therefore equivalent to 'Love all beings'. The light of reason shows us all beings, and presents them so that we may love them; the light of reason shows us what is good in every being and reveals the interior order arising from the very constitution of being.

Article 6.
Moral good is the work of the will

89. Objective good, therefore, is moral good, but becomes such only when desired by a will. As long as good is only an object of the mind, standing before the intelligence to be contemplated but not yet desired by a will that knows it, it has not attained the nature and title of moral good.

Knowledge of good has no moral connotations as long as it remains speculative and sterile in the subject possessing it. Only when the subject *wills* the good which he *knows* does good as willed begin to be moral good.

90. The will is the power with which the intelligent subject[41] works to become author of his own actions. Without the subject's will, a long series of phenomena, of which he is not the cause, can take place in him, as though he were a spectator of what occurs; not everything that happens in us is done by us. If our will is not engaged in what is happening, other powers and forces work in us but without our active intervention. Only the will provides actions that we characterise as *our own*, and use to fulfil our human *personality*. We cannot be morally good if we are not the cause and authors of the moral good attributed to us and predicated of us. The will is the active power of human intelligence; moral good is, in the final analysis, 'the objective good known by the intelligence and desired by the will.' Moral good, therefore, consists in the relationship between objective good and the will. Its notion has been clarified.

---

[41] St. Thomas says: 'The object of the will determines the act of the will by acting as a formal principle,' that is, it is essentially active, imparting and prescribing the movement. According to St. Thomas, the formal principle moving the will is *being*, the same *being* that is the object of the intellect. He then adds: *Primum autem principium formale est* ENS *et verum universale, quod est obiectum intellectus: et ideo*, he concludes, *isto modo motionis intellectus movet voluntatem, sicut praesentans ei obiectum suum* [The first formal principle is universal BEING and truth, which is the object of the intellect. Thus the intellect moves the will with this kind of movement, presenting it with its object]. *S.T.* I-II, q. 9, art. 1.

Article 7.
The order in moral good

91. There should now be no difficulty in understanding moral good as *ordered* good in such a way that the will, because it loves good, loves the order that is essentially found in good.

We have seen that:

good and being are the same;

being possesses an intrinsic *order* in its composition;

being appears to the mind as good, as soon as the mind considers it in its intrinsic, essential order;

as a consequence, good is fitting to every nature and harmonises with the interior order of each being;

the forces constituting each nature tend unceasingly to this good;

the understanding approves naturally of this good because it tends towards its object which, as being, is the seat of the order intrinsic and connatural to being; the understanding consequently tends to contemplate this harmony between things and their nature, this quasi-desire present in all things, in such a way that the harmony becomes the understanding's own good.

92. Moreover, we have seen that being and its order, and through this order the harmony between things, and between the parts of any thing, are the object and delight of intelligence and as such intelligence's good. When desired by the will, and because of its relationship with the will, this good takes on the nature and name of moral good. Human beings become morally good by using their will to become authors of the good they long for; they are pleased with what is good, and neither hate nor oppose it nor turn away from it to evil.

93. The philosophers who indicated *order* as the principle of ethics drew attention to a sublime principle. They failed, however, to discover the original source of order itself and, lacking the final explanation, were unable to justify order or sustain its necessity and authority. They had no self-evident principle to oppose to arguments against it; they were unable to discover a principle superior to order, or its source and authority, or the force of reasoning behind it. We think we

have remedied this lack of an evident principle in the moral systems, and indicated in *being*, the admirable, original source of order.

94. This seems to us the sole, legitimate way of deducing and explaining the idea of justice and uprightness. It shows the noble origin of this idea, with its roots in the first pure, evident light known to the intellect. No one can ignore this light in himself, nor exstinguish it, because it is a divine word, creating where it is uttered. We see being with our intelligence and, in being, which is all that is good, the order of being. When humans love being and love it in its order, their will is good because it loves what is good, and, loving it, renders moral what is good.

In this way, the ethical formula, 'Follow the light of reason', loses some of its vagueness. What we have said enables us to state it more precisely: 'Desire or love being, wherever you know it, in the order or degree in which it presents itself to your intelligence.'

95. There is no need to prove that the understanding knows the order of being with the act by which it knows being. This order is indistinct from being. Order constitutes the *mode* of being, if I may be permitted the word. The order of being is being as it is, neither more nor less, and hence as it is conceived by the intelligence which conceives all that is, as it is. This order, conceived by the intelligence along with being, the object of the act of intelligence, is first discovered and manifested in each contemplated object (although reflection soon analyses and distinguishes elements within the object without destroying its lasting, indivisible unity). The harmony, qualities, and accidents of being are seen in the object, together with the object's essence or foundation, as it were, and with everything else that, resting upon the foundation, develops from the essence. And order is also beheld in many objects conceived simultaneously and placed in relationship to one another.

96. There is no doubt that the intelligence weighs and measures the different degrees of being (wherever being is) in the act by which it perceives being. In the same way, the intelligence weighs and measures different degrees of good and consequently orders all good for itself according to merit,

distinguishing the greater from the lesser and giving the former priority. This is the meaning of 'to determine the order of being.'

97. For example, it is evident to the intelligence that a being without feeling is inferior to a being which feels. The intelligence sees that the non-sensitive being does not exist to itself, and hence lacks the mode of being possessed by any being that feels. It judges that a being which feels has a nobler degree of existence, and that non-sensitive being, deprived as it is of sensitive activity, is minimal in comparison. In the same way, the intelligence has only to perceive on the one hand a being which feels, and on the other an intellective being, to compare them in an immediate, easy judgment, and discover that the latter is far superior to the former. The sentient being is unknown to itself, and consequently nothing in the order of knowledge; the intellective being knows that it exists and feels, and in doing so possesses a third activity or mode additional to the other two. Another and better way of making the comparison is to consider the excellence of understanding. In virtue of his intelligence, the subject has an act of being that reaches out, it would seem, to the infinite, uniting itself with being in general. By this union, the subject is informed by and shares in an infinite capacity, that is, the capacity for the infinite. All these judgments are made easily by the mind through the notion of being, with which it perceives and measures, as we said, the various degrees and modes of being, and understands the different relationships that subsistent natures have with this first notion.

98. The intelligence soon develops its judgments. After having perceived different subsistent beings and compared them through judgments which assign to each its own degree of dignity and excellence, it can easily measure and know the various degrees of moral goodness or depravity in a will that loves or hates these beings. The goodness of the will depends upon the dignity of being as loved and the intensity with which the will loves it; its depravity depends on the dignity of being as hated, and on the intensity of the will's hate. The quantity of being as loved or hated, and the quantity of the intensity of the love or hatred are the two elements necessary for judging the morality of the will. The intellect in posses-

sion of these general norms can judge the moral actions springing from love or hatred of the different beings to which they refer.

99. In making these judgments, however, the intelligence is soon forced to take into account particular cases requiring particular norms dependent upon the general norms. The dependent rules are seen explicitly when different applications of the general norms are needed. For example, a case may arise presenting a collision between the good of two beings, and therefore between two goods in direct contradiction with one another. In such a case, what is favourable to one being is unfavourable to the other. When the collision takes place, it is already clear from the general principle, 'moral good resides in love of objective being', that 'being' must be loved as far as possible. Consequently, greater being must be loved in preference to lesser being, and greater good in preference to lesser good. We have to conclude, therefore, that lesser good must be abandoned for greater if the greater quantity of being is to be loved as far as possible. We must also conclude that love of lesser good in preference to greater, which necessarily includes rejection of what is greater, is not true love of being and good, but an illusion of love. In reality, it is effective hatred and immorality. Finally, we must conclude that desiring and reaching out for lesser good to the disregard of greater good is not desire and attainment of moral good, but desire and attainment of moral evil.

100. Observations of this kind show clearly that a morally good act tends towards being without excluding any of it, and therefore tends necessarily to the order found in being. Destroying or changing the order means putting a limitation to being. It means refusing to love being in its entirety and totality because being, intrinsically and essentially ordered, is the seat and primary source of every order.

We have to conclude that moral good contains order. In fact, moral good is being, desired for its own sake by the will; and when the will seeks being alone, it necessarily finds that order which, as we said, is only the modality of being itself.

Article 8.
Morally good acts always have the good of intelligent being as their end, and tend to the absolute

101. In order to be good, the will must hate nothing, love everything and love it in its natural order. But what is this order of good and of being?

We have seen that non-intelligent beings have existence relative to intelligent beings only, for whom they serve as means. It is therefore impossible for love in an intelligent being to be directed towards or be fulfilled in non-intelligent beings. Intelligent beings possess a certain infinite dignity raising them above irrational beings, and enabling them alone to be considered as 'ends' for a good will. In fact, the *personality* of intelligent beings, that is, everything noble in human nature and generally speaking, in intelligent natures, is constituted by this conceptual relationship with 'end' which is proper to intelligent beings.[42]

Acts of will, therefore, must have what is good in intelligences as their final aim, and cannot be at rest until they have come to love this good. These acts follow acts posited by the intellect which amongst its objects of knowledge views as *ends* only beings endowed with the noble character impressed by the light of understanding. All other beings exist relatively to the beings they serve.

102. At this point a series of questions presents itself. What is the source of this dignity possessed by intelligent natures? What is it that enables them to be considered as ends? Why is it that when we think of them, we find ourselves necessarily engaged with something so great and absolute that we can in a certain sense go no further? Why do we rest in them and love them for themselves, or rather for something supreme and final found in them that obliges our love to end in them? What is this divine element that enhances these beings, taking them beyond their own limits and allowing them to reach out towards the infinite?

---

[42] It serves no purpose to give a complete, exact definition of personality at this point. I have attempted to do so in my work *An Anthropology in aid of Moral Science*.

103. Answers to these questions are contained in what we have already said about human dignity when we spoke of universal being, present to rational natures and enlightening them with its own spark of divine fire. Because intellectual beings understand universal being, they can think, and go on thinking about particular beings until their natural progress reaches the absolute. It is through the idea of *universal being* that they are ordered towards *absolute being*.

Because of this perfect universality, the idea has an infinite extension, and bestows an infinite capacity upon its subject. The presence of this idea in human beings produces an extraordinary paradox in nature, causing us to marvel at the obvious limitations and the infinite greatness found in the human subject who is indeed formed of finite and infinite elements that alone explain the essential struggle in which human nature is perpetually involved. Seen from the point of view of man-as-subject, there is nothing weaker or more miserable than human nature; seen from the point of view of being-as-object, there is nothing greater or more noble than human nature whose intellect beholds in being its essential light from which it receives the intellectual vision of the intelligible, essential notion common to all that the subject understands.

104. Moreover, only the *absolute* itself can be that *universal being* which activates thought — not however in the state of possibility in which it now presents itself to the human mind, but in the state of perfect actuality, as it would be if the mind were to see being no longer in its initial state, as it does now, but in its subsistence as final term. Then the intellect would be perfectly replete, enraptured and enthralled: it would see God.

105. Human dignity, therefore, which exalts us above the entire feelable universe, springs from absolute, infinite being towards which we, as intelligent subjects, are ordered. When we consider ourselves from this point of view, we become cognisant of our divine excellence, and realise where our end and ultimate aim lies. The will can seek nothing better than absolute being because thought cannot pass beyond it.

But it also becomes clear that we are not ends to ourselves, although we can and must say that our end is outlined, or rather initiated in us. We realise that human nature possesses finality only in the sense that it contains in itself the beginning of the supreme end. When we love this better part of human nature, the apex of what is, love is perfectly good, perfectly moral. Then being is loved, and loved completely in its order as we reach out towards the very source of order, and towards the being in which and through which all beings are and remain.

Article 9.
The twofold dignity of moral good

106. What we have said explains the dignity attributed to morality throughout the ages, and the supreme honour and authority attributed to justice and rectitude by all peoples. But this dignity can be considered either from the point of view of *moral theory* or *in practice*, that is, in the acts of a person who acts morally.

107. Moral theory contains a twofold explanation of this dignity, dependent upon the sublime *beginning* and *end* of moral legislation which starts in *being seen by the mind* and ends in *absolute being*. Mental being is eternal, necessary, universal, inflexible: it stands above everything else. Absolute being is the fulfilment and actuation of mental being, complete, self-subsistent, the first, infinite substance, God himself.

108. In practice, there is also a twofold explanation of the dignity and intrinsic merit of morally good acts: they have their origin in intelligent beings, and terminate in intelligent beings. As we have seen, every moral act, in order truly to be such, must be an act of love having as its term some being endowed with intelligence.

109. The dignity of the author of moral acts and the dignity of their aim and term are the two reasons explaining the honour in which the conscience of all peoples holds these acts.

Article 10.
Moral legislation expressed more perfectly

110. We must now try to improve our formulation of moral legislation. We began with a vague, indetermined expression which we gradually perfected. Initially we said: 'Follow the light of reason.'

We then saw that the light of reason is being as known, and that the will is the moral faculty making human beings authors of their own actions. As a result, we were able to convert the first formula into the following: 'The will must tend towards being', that is, must love being wherever it finds it, must love every being as such.

111. But by nature being has the intrinsic character of order, and we concluded that because loving being entails loving as much being as possible, being must be loved *according to its order*. On this basis, we re-formulated our expression of moral law to take account of the necessary order in which being is to be loved if our love is to be morally good: 'The will must tend towards being according to the order found in being.'

112. Finally, we investigated the order of being, and found that amongst beings, *persons* are known as *ends*, and *things* as *means*. The will, we said, must terminate its act of love in persons. If it were content with things, its act would not be completed, nor be perfectly good, because the will would not be perfectly adapted to the nature and order of being. The end and term of its act would not be found in a final, ultimate being. With this in mind, we brought the moral formula to a higher degree of perfection by adding to it the final tendency of the will to love intelligent beings, and to rest in love of *persons*, not of *things*.

113. Our last step brought us to see what gives intelligent beings the nature of 'end' relative to the will. We contemplated the divine, unconditioned, infinite element in intelligent beings and saw how it longs to complete itself in them by revealing to them its subsistence, its majesty as God. By separating this truly final, infinite element from every other condition on which the subject depends, we saw that a perfectly good and sound will must have as the final point of

desire this wonderful principle underlying intelligence and happiness. The will has to love relatively to this term, beyond which nothing exists, and in this term consummate all its longings. Only in this way does the will truly love being as it is. It loves *per se*, being which is *per se*. Relative to this being, it loves all other beings which are not *per se*, but related to first, essential being.

5

THE WILL AS THE CAUSE OF MORAL GOOD AND EVIL

Article 1.
The nature of the will

114. As we have seen, the will is our interior, moral power. 'Good' is called 'moral good' when it is desired by a will. Properly speaking, *morality* is 'a relationship between what is good and the intelligent nature which wills the good'.

The morally good act consists in willing good, or being, and it is this act which we must now examine with the utmost attention. Already we have indicated it rather vaguely, using various phrases to describe it: to will is, 'to tend towards being', 'to love being', 'to desire being'. These phrases must be rendered more accurate and definite by a careful analysis of the morally good act posited by an intelligent subject.

115. First we must determine the nature of the will. Is it our only power for action, and if not how is it distinguished from other active powers within us?

We recall that the human being has two principal passive faculties, feeling and intelligence. *Feeling* enables us to perceive things as subsistent; *intelligence* is our power of conceiving things mentally in so far as they are possible. The understanding conceives objectively, reaching out to things as objects of the mind and hence as essentially different from the subject; feeling perceives things subjectively, through the action they exert in the subject which they modify.

116. These two passive faculties are accompanied by two active powers: *instinct* corresponds to feeling, *will* corresponds to intelligence. Instinct moves the subject towards pleasurable things and presides over the subject's happiness;[43] will is the subject moving itself[44] to approve known objects in

---

[43] Just as there are two *senses* in us, the corporeal and the spiritual, there are also two *instincts*. The first moves us to bodily *pleasure*, the second moves us continually to *happiness*.

[44] For this reason we said earlier that human personality has its proper place in the will because, although instinct is an active power, it cannot be

so far as they can be approved, without reference to the subject itself or to the pure delight consequent upon this approval. It is the will that presides over rectitude or moral good.

117. The will, therefore, is the active power by which human beings operate relatively to the objects of their mind rather than according to the stimulus of inclination. Through the will, the subject operates knowingly and in accord with the reasons he contemplates.

Article 2.
Free will reveals itself as human beings reflect

118. We define the will as an 'active power operating according to reasons present to the mind and proposed by the human subject to himself'. It is clear therefore that the will depends upon prior cognitions in order to act; human beings must have first acquired ideas that can then serve as reasons enabling them to deliberate, choose and will.

119. The knowledge present in the subject before his will acts is formed instinctively, not willingly. This *direct* knowledge[45] then becomes the matter, or (as I would prefer to say) the object and aim of *reflection*. The act which precedes the act of will, is a first act instinctively moving the subject to perception and other acts of knowledge.[46] As a result of remembering his perceptions and the ideas of things, the subject, drawn now not by instinct but by a principle of reason, can reflect upon them willingly. The desire of profit, for example, cannot be a motivating power in business if we do not know what profit is; the idea of profit must be present to the mind if the will is going to desire it as an end. Without such an idea, profit could not be an end for human activity; and if we could not propose it to ourselves as an end, we

---

considered as an intelligent subject using a power; on the contrary it is a power functioning in the intelligent subject.

[45] I have spoken at length about direct knowledge in *Certainty*, 1149-1157, 1258 ss.

[46] *The Origin of Thought*, 524.

could not will it. It is the nature of the will to work for an end, and to use only what is known as a motive or reason for action: *voluntas non fertur in incognitum* ['the will is not drawn to what it does not know']

120. When we decide to work for an end, such as profit, we need to present it to our mind in order to will it. In other words, we have to reflect upon an idea which we already possess, draw it from our habitual memory and fix our attention upon it so that it is *actually* present to us and becomes a target-sign for our will. The whole process of willing consists in first having the idea (direct knowledge) of what we are going to will, before reflecting upon it in order to make it an object of willing.

121. The difference and contrast between simply *knowing* something and *willing* it does not require successive acts in the human subject. Nevertheless it is certain that the two operations very often do succeed one another, that the act of knowledge is distinct from the act of will, and that this second act is dependent upon the first in the sense that human beings can will only what they know. It is also certain, to the acute observer, that by his act of will a subject *adheres* to what is desired as the term of his volition. But adhering to what is known is equivalent to reflecting upon an idea, upon the thing as known. An act of will is an act of reflection terminating not in simple contemplation, but in 'assenting' contemplation. Reflection may take place without any desire for what is known and reflected upon, but it can also terminate in an act of will. If so, will is found at the term or final point of reflection where what is already known in the idea and held in the memory as a result of perception is now beheld anew.

122. The close connection between *reflection* and the *will* may also be illustrated by reference to matters explained elsewhere.

123. The act of reflection with which we turn our attention to things known to us through direct knowledge either effects something in what is known or effects and produces nothing. In the second case, reflection simply looks at things as they present themselves, reinforcing its attention by making them more vivid and actual, but without producing any new cognition. In the first case, however, reflection analyses, unites or

integrates[47] previous direct knowledge, and thus becomes a source of new knowledge. The new forms and aspects under which the mind considers what it has known previously are themselves new knowledge.

Where reflection is at work to draw new knowledge from what the subject already knows, the term of reflection is increased knowledge; where reflection simply fixes attention more vividly on what is known, it may terminate either by beholding knowledge anew or by willing it also, that is, by assenting willingly to the truth and goodness of what is known.

With the act of will, therefore, the intelligent subject reflects upon something he knows (which forms part of direct knowledge), and terminates his act by *assenting* to it. In other words, he acknowledges what he knows as good by desiring and willing it.

124. There are, therefore, three types of reflective acts. The first is simply contemplation of what is already known; it offers no new knowledge, nor is it a volition. The second analyses, unites and integrates things already known; it produces new knowledge, but without volition. The third and last beholds anew the known object, willingly draws pleasure from it, enjoys it, and rejoices in the delight experienced by an intelligent being who fully *acknowledges* the good present in what is known. This third kind of reflection is *volition*, and implies abandonment on the part of the willing subject to the pleasing action raised in the mind by all things desired as they should be.

125. We can now ask: what causes reflection? what stimulates or motivates a person to pass to a reflective from a non-reflective state? One sufficient reason for this passage is found in *instinct*, another in the *will* (it is not impossible for one act of will to be dependent upon a preceding volition: a person can will to will).

126. But whatever causes reflection upon what we know, it is certain that the conclusion of our reflection — the term, the final judgment, the assent, the repose of spirit that comprises the act of will — depends upon ourselves. This explains how

---

[47] For the integrating faculty of the understanding see *The Origin of Thought*, 623-624.

the human person operates through the will, and it allows us to define the act of will as 'a final act consummating, not initiating, reflection'. It is, therefore, an act carried out with knowledge of its cause and preceded by an inchoate reflection which is not yet an act of will. Only when it pleases us to add volition to reflection as a complement and conclusion does reflection share the nature of volition.

Article 3.
How actions and affections depend upon the will

127. When I voluntarily carry out an action, I show that I prefer to do it rather than not do it; I have preferred that action to all the others I could have chosen. If I had not chosen it (I cannot be *forced* to do it because the action in question is voluntary, not simply physical), I would have declined it; if another action had presented itself which I preferred, I would have done it.

128. What does this observation about the strict connection between *actions* and *affections* show us? It enables us to grasp this important truth: we always act in dependence upon our predominant love. It would be absurd to think of abandoning something we love more for the sake of something we love less. In every case without exception the true sign and expression of our love is found in our actions because they are in some way an effect of our love. We could, for example, imagine ourselves morally forced to do something we do not like ('morally', because the actions of the will are not subject to mechanical violence or necessity). Fear, for instance, can exert great pressure upon us. But it remains true that what we do in such a case is a consequence of a prevalent affection (I am not speaking of extraordinary fear which can overwhelm the mind and leave us devoid of knowledge. This would render impossible any act of the will, and leave the field open to instinct). When a person acts willingly, he acts naturally and necessarily according to the love predominant in him at that moment. The contrary is impossible. Whatever the circumstances, whatever the fear, for example, impelling him to carry out an action he would otherwise avoid, he does at least consider his fear-motivated action as the lesser evil. But

the lesser evil, when compared with the greater, is indeed something good, and good is what he loves; in these circumstances a person does not choose evil as such, but as a means of freedom from the greater evil he fears more. From this point of view, the lesser evil becomes lovable, although in other ways it may be detested.

129. We must also notice that the predominant love with which we act is very different from all other love and endowed with special characteristics. In other words, it is not speculative, but *practical* love. It is not love in general, but a particular love in which we consider in detail the action we have to perform. It is not habitual love, nor does it necessarily last for a long time; it is actual love, and as such may last only for the instant immediately preceding and determining our action. Very often we find ourselves drawn by spontaneous love to do something we had previously condemned and which we regret as soon as it has been done. As the poet says,
 'An instant served to thrust us down.'
  [Dante, *Commedia*, Inferno 6]
The intensity of the love lasts only for the instant in which it is decided upon, but in this very instant we are moved to act. Love for something else may prevail immediately afterwards.

130. Thus we become mysteries to ourselves, living contradictions who immediately disavow what we have just willed. We marvel at the brevity of such acts of love in which we do something we may have previously despised. They occur so quickly that we neither know nor examine them, and they easily escape our advertence. Actions like these enfold and hide the many, swift gradations by which passion takes root, grows strong and finally arrives at its term, ready, unless we oppose it with some greater love, to expand and stimulate our effective powers and exterior actions.

131. There is no doubt, therefore, that an act of love will necessarily produce its desired effect if stimulated strongly enough before another act intervenes. Under such stimulation, freedom is no longer present or (as I would prefer to say) the willing subject has irrevocably brought the act of freedom to its conclusion.

132. All the actions of moral beings are brought about by an act of predominant love, which I call *practical love*. When

this love has been posited, action follows necessarily. On the other hand, the human subject is free. Where is his free will to be found? In his *actions*? Or in the way he determines the *love* with which alone a moral agent produces his actions?

133. It cannot consist in actions willed independently of love because to will actions without loving them involves contradiction. But if we are free to will or not to will our actions, we do so because we are free to love them or not, free to increase or diminish our love or hatred for any actions or omissions. The power we call *freedom* is first exercised on the affections of our heart and only consequently on our actions in so far as they are inseparably bound to our affections. Our actions are free, but only by sharing in the freedom present in our affections.

134. Granted that we rule our actions solely because we rule our affections, we have to see if freedom has its origin in the affections. Are we free simply because we are free in governing our affections, or do the affections themselves depend upon a previous operation of our spirit just as our external actions depend upon the affections?

135. If we examine the nature of human affections, and of love and hatred in particular, we find that we can hate something only if we think it bad — it is impossible for good to cause hatred in us. Similarly, we cannot love anything unless we consider it good because evil cannot cause love in us. It is true, of course, that we can love what is harmful and bad for us, but only on condition that we view it under a favourable aspect enabling us to judge it good. Similarly I can hate things useful and good for me, but only if I consider them from a displeasing and harmful point of view. Love and hatred are not aroused in me by the thing as it is in itself, but by the way in which I consider, think and judge it. The thing may be good, but if I judge and consider it bad, I will reject it; it may be bad, but if I judge and consider it good, it will attract my love. As the scholastics said, evil can be loved by us only *sub specie boni* [when it appears good]. Like so many other sayings of the schoolmen, this has passed into everyday language because it expresses a feeling common to us all.

136. We must remember that love, as an affection proper to an intelligent being, is directed towards a known object

which, revealing its worth to the mind, causes affection and love in the knowing subject. *Esteem* is an intrinsic element of *love*, which is not to be confused with blind, material instinct. If I love an object, I necessarily esteem and approve it as pleasing and good, and worthy of love. I cannot love it without first esteeming it because love depends upon a favourable judgment about the worth and lovable qualities of the object. It is true that while I love an object, I also know its defects, but these are not the aim and cause of my love. The object must possess some real or apparent worth attracting my love while weakening or extinguishing the aversion produced by its defects. The act may be momentary, as we said, and I may disapprove of it immediately, but for that moment love of the object has prevailed. I have found a powerful reason for loving the object; I have been struck by its worth and blinded to everything else; I have esteemed it as lovable and as such held it dear. For a single instant I have been dominated by it, and in that instant have necessarily esteemed what I know while I love it (I assume that it is love, not irrational frenzy). I have persuaded myself of the overwhelming worth of the object which I have been drawn to desire.

137. Love, therefore, is immediately preceded by esteem, which produces it; a judgment about the worth and lovableness of the object loved indicates love as the act of an intelligent being, and distinguishes it from animal inclinations which are confined to bodily sensibility and unrelated to freedom. Esteem and judgment in this case are called *practical esteem* and *practical judgment*, to distinguish them from other kinds of esteem and judgment. *Practical* denotes the kind of judgment we make about the worth of the things we perceive. It is the efficient cause or at least condition of every affection, and the immediate, necessary step preceding it.

138. Practical love, therefore, is produced by practical esteem and is not to be confused with speculative esteem rising from general, stable reasons. Practical esteem can depend upon very particular reasons, and is sometimes based on momentary incidents. And love exists only when enkindled by preceding, practical esteem as its necessary source. On the other hand, as soon as we have arrived at our practical

esteem for a being, and judged it practically, love springs up inevitably as a continuation of our esteem, and as a feeling of esteem.

Love and esteem are bound together by an unchangeable law not dependent on human deliberation. In this respect their bond is similar to that between external actions and love. Only by first increasing or diminishing our practical esteem for an object can we increase or lessen our love for it; only through esteem can we influence our love by our power of free will; only because we increase or lessen in ourselves the practical esteem we have for an object's worth are we able to increase or lessen our love, which is intimately and essentially tied to esteem as an effect is bound to its cause.

139. Human freedom, therefore, is exercised primarily, immediately and properly on the esteem or *practical judgment* that we bring to bear on the objects we contemplate mentally. Our affections, love and hatred are influenced only mediately. The nature and laws of freedom are to be sought in the first act of reflection on the objects present to our mind by which we form our esteem or practical judgment. Our next step, therefore, is to examine carefully this first act of reflection.

140. We have already distinguished *direct* from *reflex* knowledge and shown that while the former is necessary, the latter depends upon human will. The practical judgment we are describing is simply an act of reflection upon things already perceived. We know these things, and we form a judgment about them through the ideas that give us knowledge of them. But the whole process by which this operation is carried out by the willing spirit requires acute observation and careful charting as we shall see.

Direct knowledge is necessary knowledge; it does not depend upon an act of will.

This statement is explained by noting that direct knowledge is the result of our first ideas about things. Before we acquire these ideas, we have no special interest stimulating any kind of desire for them — we do not even know them. We do not perceive them deliberately, but instinctively and passively, as they present themselves. For example, before I know what human beings are, I cannot esteem them, nor judge whether they please or displease me. I have no motive drawing me favourably or unfavourably to the idea, human being; I receive it just as it is. But after I have come to know what someone is, and formed the idea of human beings, I can evaluate them in various ways, looking at them as good or bad, deserving of love or hate. First I must have the idea; then I can form my judgment. The idea provides *direct knowledge* which is not, and cannot be, subject to my will, and hence cannot be the source of morality.

141. But given the idea, or direct knowledge, our reflection upon the idea can be wholly voluntary. With full deliberation we can now judge what we know, and lead our reflection to a conclusion which conforms with our will.

In the idea of the thing (direct knowledge), I have mentally conceived the being of the thing. I have also conceived the being as good because being is good and the foundation of what is good. If I now wish to note explicitly the quantity of good in this thing, it is sufficient to note its quantity of being. I already know this quantity as it is because I have conceived directly the thing I know. If I want to note what it is I have conceived, or affirm to myself its degree of being or level of goodness, it is sufficient for me to reflect upon what I know and acknowledge it (re-know it, re-cognise it) without hiding from myself what it is, and what I already know it to be. Full, entire *acknowledgement* (re-cognition) of what I already *know*, that is, of the objects already perceived by me, is an act immediately subject to my free will. The moral act begins here, and is formed here. *Love* and *external action* follow as its effects.

142. To remove equivocation and confusion in describing this highly important operation of the human spirit, which we easily lose sight of, we have to note the difference between the effect of sensation and the effect of direct knowledge. *Sensation* produces in us an instinctive inclination towards or aversion from the objects we feel; *ideas*, on the contrary, are universal[48] by nature and frigid, and produce only an

---

[48] The *idea* of a thing is simply the intuition of the *possibility of the thing*, and the possibility of a thing is by nature cold. *Possible food* does not appease hunger and does not interest the starving. The same is true of every good that is merely possible.

incipient, uniform delight which would cease immediately without the intervention of willing reflection. This reflection acts upon the first ideas we have of things. It contemplates them, adheres to them and cherishes the worth of the objects it thinks of, drawing from it the delight dependent upon willing reflection which allows us to feel and intellectually enjoy the efficacy of this worth. It is not the first idea of a thing which produces living delight in us; reflection enamours us of what we know and gives rise to our loving adherence to what we know. But embracing a known object in order to sense its worth is a voluntary act of the spirit; the spirit throws light for itself upon the object and, by predisposing itself to receive more effectively the impression of this idea and likeness, perceives it more vividly. The light accumulating on the object and its worth — if this is the aim of the act of reflection — draws the will to ever greater degrees of delight which lead in their turn to true, increasing levels of endearment.

143. The first ideas in which things are known to us are all equally cold, and provide light without warmth. The will, therefore, remains perfectly free, and its first act consists in reaching out to acknowledge or disavow the worth of things. If the will acts with the intention of acknowledging the being's worth, it reflectively fixes its attention on what it knows, and allows the worth of what it knows to work vividly within it. The will unveils for itself greater, more enhancing and enthralling light which leads it to judge favourably and practically what it knows. If the will acts with the intention of disavowing its objects of knowledge, it either admires their worth slightly or fixes its gaze on their defects by putting its objects in the least favourable light. Seen like this, their deformities and defects become obvious and produce a displeasing feeling with proportionate hatred and external actions towards the objects themselves.

144. The process by which the human will operates can, therefore, be described as follows. First, ideas and memories of things are found as direct knowledge in human beings. The will then prompts reflection on what is known. This reflection is either morally good or bad in so far as the worth of

these things are impartially acknowledged, or disavowed and distorted.

145. If the will is good, that is, free from self-interest, secondary ends and perverse instincts, its sole aim is to acknowledge known things for what they actually are, with all their good properties and defects. In this case, the will moves naturally towards the *truth* without exaggerating the action of defects relative to that of good properties, or insisting upon some defects and good properties rather than others. What is known is loved in all its parts, as it is; no wrong is done to it because all the being found in it is loved without exaggeration or diminution.

146. A bad will does not aim at truth. Stimulated by an evil instinct,[49] this kind of will fixes its reflection partially and unjustly on the objects of the mind (direct knowledge) and disposes itself towards disorder by accepting a disproportionate stimulus either from the defects or good properties of what it knows. In the first case, it is prey to irrational and unjust hatred, in the second to irrational and unjust love.

147. The origin of irrational hatred depends upon the will's decision to turn away from the good properties of the thing it knows and devote its attention to the thing's defects; irrational love involves complete attention to the good properties and disregard for the defects. But the power inherent in voluntary reflection goes further than this. This power is capable of creating imaginary defects in the thing it knows if this thing is the object of its hatred, and imaginary good properties if it wishes to love the known object unduly. This power of will is an extremely important fact, and is always underestimated.

148. However, from what has been said it is clear that the will is perfectly free when it begins to reflect upon the objects perceived, and is able then either to acknowledge in simplicity the things known through direct knowledge (things present in the mind), or disavow them. In the first case, the will is good; in the second, evil. Moral goodness or evil has its proper seat, therefore, in the first voluntary direction taken by reflection.

---

[49] Action of the will is always present when we act for a known end. But instinct can also move us for the same end. Hence both will and instinct intermingle and often act together.

Its source and origin lies here and accounts for the words spoken by the author of the gospel, 'When your eye is sound, your whole body is full of light; but when it is not sound, your body is full of darkness'.[50] The eye of the soul is healthy when the will, seeing clearly, stimulates sound desires and actions done in the perfection of light. In fact, the will exerts itself rightly or wrongly in the act of reflection. It adheres to what it desires, and in doing this produces for itself a *vital apprehension* of the worth or defect of the things present to it. This *vital apprehension* is true or false because the will has the power to see what is not actually present in the thing known, just as it can also decide, if it so wishes, not to see what is actually there. Vital apprehension of good or evil in the thing concludes with practical judgment or esteem for what is known, that is, in faithful or unfaithful *acknowledgement* of what has been perceived in direct knowledge. This is the ground of moral *consent*.

149. Once this acknowledgement, or practical judgment and esteem, has been formed, *vital pleasure* or *displeasure* immediately arises to accompany the *vital apprehension* of good or evil. Pleasure then gives rise to love, which is formed immediately as the final complement to pleasure; displeasure gives rise to hatred, its seal and complement. Love and hatred are followed by action.

150. Before a moral being arrives at his external action, therefore, the spirit works inwardly according to the following steps: 1st step, apprehension or *direct knowledge* of things; 2nd, *voluntary reflection* on the things known — this reflection is upright or perverse in so far as it tends to *acknowledge* faithfully the direct knowledge, or to alter it; 3rd, *meditation*, that is, the varying period in which voluntary reflection concentrates on what is known directly; 4th, *vital*, efficacious *apprehension* resulting from meditation and depending for its truth or falsehood on the upright or wayward act of will giving rise to meditation; 5th, *practical judgment* or *esteem*, the effect and complement of vital apprehension; 6th, *intellectual delight* or *pain*, the effect of the practical judgment; 7th, *practical love*; 8th, *external acts*.

---

[50] Lk 11. [34]

151. This is the series of operations, or rather successive states in a moral being who acts externally. His external action is only the last of the seven steps we have enumerated and analysed. The first is direct knowledge, immune in its formation from any act of will, but nevertheless the foundation of the moral edifice in so far as it provides the will with the matter on which to turn and exercise its activity.

152. I cannot see that it is possible for anyone turning back attentively on himself not to acknowledge the truth of the formation of the moral act, as I have described it. Nevertheless one difficulty in understanding it could easily arise, and it would be helpful to remove it immediately. How can voluntary reflection, concentrating on known things, create in them what is not present in them, or disregard what is to be seen in them? It would seem at first sight that we are not free relative to what we think, and that we must see things as we perceive them. The difficulty is easily resolved if we examine carefully the fact of knowledge as we have described it.

153. It is true that things are perceived as they present themselves, and in this way form what we call direct knowledge which, as we have said, is immune from influence of any judgment directed by the will and anterior to the use of human freedom.

But as we pass from knowing things to acknowledging them, that is, to reflecting upon things already known to us, and viewing their worth, goodness and lovableness, our will shows itself to be free. It has the capacity to alter its own knowledge and form false judgments about the things it has perceived by conceding to them good properties or defects they do not possess. And this is always the cause of error in human minds. Error is the effect of voluntary reflection; if this were not the case, error would be inexplicable. But I have spoken elsewhere at length about the will as the cause of error.[51]

154. We have to bear in mind that we not only *reason*, but *believe*. Believing in ourselves and in our passions we choose, on this basis, to form completely artificial persuasions. It is the will's power to propose things for its own belief which

---

[51] *Certainty*, 1279 ss.

lies at the root of the first interior injustice we are describing as the source and essence of every injustice and immorality.

155. Why do we find ourselves at odds about things we obviously perceive in the same way? We use the same words to name these things and understand without difficulty the common meaning we give to the words. This is sufficient to show that direct knowledge is equal for all. But a reflective judgment intervenes which varies according to the subject forming it. This judgment provides one person with one result, and another with another, according to the dispositions of will in the person making the judgment.

156. Listen, for example, to politicians discussing facts at election time. I do not mean the 'facts' they actually invent in order to deceive others rather than themselves. The judgments I refer to are those with which they deceive themselves by giving credence to what favours their hopes and opinions, and obstinately refusing to admit contrary, well-founded information; judgments which cause them to exaggerate success and lessen failure; judgments which make them careful about certain things and careless about others; judgments which draw them to examine minutely things which please them and to ignore what displeases them.

157. Ingenious arguments are conjured up by politicians to persuade themselves that all is well; a curious obtuseness draws a veil over situations they prefer to hide from themselves. People of different parties will listen together to a report on the same facts and immediately reflect on this direct knowledge in their own favour . Their will, already inclined to whatever helps their own party, prompts reflection which inevitably results in conclusions suitable to their own purposes. Statistics, for example, are notoriously prone to opposite interpretations, although there may be unqualified agreement about the numbers and percentages under discussion. It is possible, of course, that different interpretations depend upon varying degrees of intellectual capacity or foresight on the part of the interpreters, but experience shows that people are only too prone to adopt the absurd logic of others when such a tactic suits them. We can be sure that contrary conclusions exist which depend not on different starting points, nor on superior intelligence in one of the

parties, but on determination to see the matter through in one's own favour.

158. Summing up, we can say that anyone with an evil will has two standards, one for things favourable and one for things unfavourable to himself. These standards prove the power of the will to intervene in reasoning: error is not found in direct, necessary cognition, but in voluntary, reflective knowledge made up of judgment, spurious persuasion, and credulity.

Article 4.
The principle of justice consists in ACKNOWLEDGING the being we know

159. We have, therefore, an interior energy enabling us to voluntarily esteem objects we know, to form persuasions about them, and to impose our own belief on them. This is the special work of the will.

Esteem is followed by affection, which participates in the voluntariness of esteem; affection is followed by external action, which in turn depends on the voluntariness of affection. Esteem is of its nature, essentially free; affection is free but in dependence on the freedom of esteem; external action is free because it necessarily depends upon affection and shares in its freedom.

160. The persuasion and esteem we form for ourselves with the power of our reflective will is *reasonable* if it harmonises with our direct knowledge of the thing about which we form our persuasion; it is *unreasonable* if it departs from direct knowledge through the force of our own interior, *creative* effort. In this case it is imaginary, artificial and arbitrary persuasion, suitably described by the tag: *stat pro ratione voluntas* ['will takes the place of reason']. In other words, error is entirely individual, produced by ourselves alone.

This would explain the pride people take in error. We sense that it is our own work, and that we use more energy in erring than we would in simply acknowledging the truth. The greater effort required in making a mistake becomes our title to the miserable glory so many seek and so many are prepared to bestow.

161. The persuasion we are describing is always a judgment. When we persuade ourselves that an object possesses a certain degree of goodness or worth in itself, we judge that the thing really is like this. The judgment is true if it corresponds with our direct knowledge; it is false if it differs from the direct knowledge. The esteem we bestow on the thing depends upon this judgment, and is just or unjust in so far as it is proportionate to the idea or knowledge we possess of the thing. *Reasonableness* in persuasion, *truth* in judgment and *justice* in esteem are essentially the same thing, but expressed in three different relationships or modes.

162. What, then, is the final basis of the morally good act? What constitutes an upright, just act?

The moral act consists in *acknowledging* what we already *know*. We *know* things: this is direct, necessary knowledge; we *acknowledge* things: this is reflective, voluntary knowledge. In direct knowledge we mentally conceive what we know, and in what we know, all its being. If, in reflecting on what we know, we acknowledge everything contained in what we know, we necessarily affirm the just, true degree of goodness in the thing; if, with the whole thing present to our mind, we dissimulate its being, we do an injury to what we know and we lie to ourselves by judging it to have less goodness than it actually possesses. We *know* what this degree of goodness is, but we do not *want* to know what it is. And we perpetrate the same kind of lying injustice, but at a deeper level, when we voluntarily and arbitrarily place more good in what we know than the thing actually contains. We see, or we say we see, some good which is not truly present in what we know, and is not seen by us.

163. Two acts of knowledge take place within us. If they *agree*, we possess truth and justice; if they *disagree*, we have lied interiorly, we are unjust.

If our second knowledge is true and good, it consists in an *assent* given by the will to our first knowledge of a thing. The will gladly rests, as it were, in our first, spontaneous knowledge. Truth makes its home in us, and brings tranquillity and peace in its wake. If our second knowledge is false and evil, it consists in the *will's* aversion and unjust *dissent* from the first knowledge. The will refuses to acknowledge what it first knows, and rebels against truth. Instead of admitting what it knows, it tries to change the very being of things by bringing them into contrast with true, legitimate and natural knowledge, and by substituting for truth a veneer of false, imaginary and unnatural knowledge. A battle commences between what is true and a will that is averse to what is true — but the will is unable to prevent what is true from continuing to be true.

164. These observations explain why persuasion about error is always weaker than persuasion about truth. A person persuaded of error always bears deep within himself a continual contradiction of his error. Direct knowledge is never extinguished within us unless we fall into total ignorance about things.

165. The same observations explain why in certain circumstances the strongest arguments make little or no impression on certain persons whose minds are filled with endless, pointless doubts about the most evident matters. They also explain why, as the gospel says, 'seeing they may not see, and hearing they may not understand'.[52]

166. Again, these observations explain why probity, rectitude and justice bring peace to the human heart, while injustice leads to internal distress and tension. In the just person everything harmonises — the will with knowledge, direct knowledge with reflective knowledge. Injustice, however, leads to continual strife between the will and knowledge, and between reflection and direct knowledge; despite our knowledge about things, we deny its existence and refuse to adhere to it. But we cannot do this without continual violence to ourselves because we cannot destroy what is present to our spirit. We can never eliminate our grasp of what we know, nor annihilate the truth within: it continually condemns us, witnessing to our error and our immorality.

167. Finally, such observations throw greater light on what has been said about the supreme principle of morality. In the

---

[52] Lk 8. 10

last analysis, this principle consists in the voluntary ACKNOW-
LEDGEMENT of our first, necessary knowledge, that is, in not
denying what we know and in voluntarily admitting the good
present in what we have perceived. This acknowledgement
and assent is the joyful tribute of homage and esteem that we
freely and rightly pay to things we know, and to their
goodness.

Article 5.
Truth is the principle of morality

168. Truth is an exemplar or type, a norm or rule of the
mind, a standard for that which must conform to it.[53] As a
type, it is the truth of what refers to it. A thing is true if it
conforms to its truth, or type; if not, it is false.

Being is the first, universal exemplar, and the supreme rule
of every judgment. It is, therefore, the first, universal truth.

Every *idea* is truth relative to something; the thing is *true* if
it corresponds to its idea.

Direct knowledge is simply the idea of something and
hence the *truth*. Reflective judgments are *true* if they conform
with their truth or direct knowledge. They are false if they
disagree with direct knowledge because the only aim of these
judgments is to affirm that the thing I have mentally
conceived is as I have conceived it. The idea or direct
knowledge preceding reflective judgments serves as the norm
directing these judgments.

If I do not faithfully acknowledge the worth of something
known by me, but invent something to replace my
knowledge of this worth, I lie to myself. This lie is the
immoral act of which we are speaking.

169. It is clear, therefore, that *truth* is the principle of
morality, and that *acknowledgement of the truth* (that is,
acknowledgement of direct knowledge) is the supreme duty
and the proper, essential act of morality. This explains why in
scripture truth and moral goodness on the one hand, and
lying and sin on the other, are often synonymous. Every sin

---

[53] For the definition of *truth* see *Opuscoli Filosofici*, vol. 1, pp. 98, 318 ss, and, in more detail, *Certainly*, 1044 ss and 1123 ss.

is finally a way of lying to ourselves. Before positing the externally evil act, we have succeeded in deceiving and seducing ourselves internally. A false, lying interior word is the foundation of all our exterior misdemeanours.

170. The upright person, dear to the Lord, is described with great wisdom in the scriptures as one who 'speaks truth in his heart'.[54] God's law itself is 'truth'.[55]

Article 6.
How the force of obligation is made known within us

171. We have examined our power of will and seen that it either surrenders to the truth or substitutes for the truth a lie which it respects as though it were the truth. But when I have the idea of something (direct knowledge), and disavow its worth to myself, I esteem the thing falsely and unjustly. At that moment, I feel I am doing what is wrong. I feel *remorse*, and become aware of my own impropriety. This remorse, and consciousness of impropriety, makes known the *force of obligation*.

172. When I know something (with direct knowledge), nothing forces me to tell myself that I do not know it, nor to affirm that my knowledge is different from what it actually is. My reflection simply tells me that what I know has a certain nature and being, together with certain degrees of being and a certain worth superior to something else. In other words, I declare that I know the thing in a certain way. I am giving myself an account of my own knowledge and saying that on reflection I find that what I know has these degrees and modes of being which make it superior in worth to something else. My esteem for the thing is founded only on the previous knowledge I have of it. Esteem is simply an analysis by which I voluntarily confirm and declare what I already know. It is, in a word, an acknowledgement.

173. It is obvious, however, that if I deny my knowledge of what I actually know, I lie to myself. Nothing forces me to

---

[54] *Qui loquitur veritatem in corde suo.* Ps. 14. [3. He that speaks truth in his heart. *Douai*].
[55] *Lex tua veritas.* Ps. 118. [142. Thy law is the truth. *Douai*].

tell myself that I know something in one way if I do not know it in that way. I am voluntarily lying to myself through the internal power by which I can either assent gracefully to what I know by acknowledging it, or hatefully rebel against it either by refusing to acknowledge what I know or by refusing to tell myself that I know what I do indeed know — whether I want to acknowledge it or not.

174. It is clearly *fitting* that I should both affirm to myself what I know exactly as I know it, and witness to my knowledge without changing or deforming it; it is clearly *unfitting* that I should do the opposite. The fittingness that I feel about acting in this way is the *first* moral *obligation*. It is perfectly obvious, and the reason and source of all other obligations; it is the form of what is *upright*, just as unfittingness forms moral *impropriety*.

175. I want to insist that the *obligation* of acknowledging what one knows is evident *per se* in my first reflective operation. It does not need proof, because I cannot know a thing and tell myself I do not know it without precipitating an internal contradiction and tension from which spring the unfittingness that constitutes evil.[56] I become the *author* of the evil within me because I voluntarily make myself the author of my interior contradiction and tension, that is, of the struggle between acknowledgement and knowledge. As the willing author of evil in an intelligent being, I make myself morally bad.

176. The interior contradiction and tension that I cause for myself when I create and imagine for myself a reflective knowledge contrary to direct knowledge is alien to the order of being. Order is synonymous with harmony and concord, and has its source in the intimate exigency of direct knowledge, the type to which reflective knowledge must conform. Direct knowledge is unchangeable. It is truth itself, as we said, and outside any action of the human will, As such, it requires by its very nature to be acknowledged for what it is, and not to be disavowed.

There is no need to prove that if we want to affirm what we know, we have to affirm what we do in fact know. We are

[56] Chap. 2, art. 2.

now at the level of the principle of identity and have brought ethics to its primary reason where the principle of morality is fully evident. If we affirm that we do not know what we do indeed know, or if we affirm that we do know what we do not know, are we not endeavouring to make something what it is not, or not what it is? In this case we are acting contrary to the principle of contradiction which affirms, 'that which is, cannot not be, and that which is not, cannot be.' Our attack is on *being* itself as we struggle to make it not what it is, or make it what it is not. Our will has rebelled, and turned on truth and being, in order to destroy them. It desires evil because it attempts as far as it can to overthrow *truth* and *being* and to destroy *good* along with them. This violent outrage on the part of our will is the essence of immorality.

Article 7.
An objection overcome

177. It may be objected that I cause human freedom to act without a sufficient reason. But how, I ask, does this sufficient reason determine the human will? If it determines the will necessarily, the will cannot operate freely. Free will is destroyed. But if it determines the will while leaving it free to act or not, human freedom has been safeguarded — which is the teaching I have developed throughout this book.

In fact it is false to say that I make the will act without sufficient reason. On the contrary, I define the will as a power of acting which follows a reason. This is the will's specific characteristic, and distinguishes it from pure instinct. But I go on to note that when the will has several reasons for acting, it can of its own acord choose to render them more or less effective for itself by making some prevail through the use of the practical judgment we have spoken of. The will never acts without a reason, but this reason is weighed by the will itself and prevails because the balance has been tilted in its favour. The will either allows itself to be moved by this reason, or resists it freely by bringing forward another reason.

178. Let us look a little more carefully at human actions. We involuntarily receive perceptions and ideas of things

(direct knowledge). When we act to evaluate what we know, we realise that we must not conceal from ourselves anything we know. We feel obliged to acknowledge simply and purely the known truth. This truth — the things known to us — is the reason according to which we *know* we have to judge. Consequently we *feel* an obligation to carry out our judgment uprightly. But some self-interest, dependent upon feeling, may intervene (initially by chance, perhaps), or pride may interfere, to make us think that it would be useful to disavow what we know. We may be drawn to judge what we know in a different way from that in which we know it. A new reason has presented itself, and our spirit is now face to face with contrary reasons: one of them tells us to surrender to truth and probity; the other to pursue pleasure by rebelling against the truth and disavowing it.

We know that we must follow the first reason; we feel its intimate fittingness and its absolute, unchangeable obligation.

179. Nevertheless, neither this obligation nor the delight opposed to it impels us mechanically to action. We are *free*, and can act either according to the obligation we feel, or disregard our duty and second our guilty inclination. We decide between good and evil; we make the choice. In doing so we form our practical judgment which prefers to accept or reject our obligation. In the first case we act uprightly; in the second we sin.

180. The efficacy of our will lies in this practical judgment. In either case we act for a reason, but in practice by choosing the reason we want. The choice we make depends upon the interior efficacy of the will itself, the wonderful power we use to move ourselves rather than be moved. The will is a kind of creative power that we employ to complete sufficient reason, as scripture says in describing human freedom. God 'made man from the beginning, and left him in the hand of his own counsel.[57] He added his commandments and precepts. If you will keep the commandments and perform acceptable fidelity for ever, they will preserve you. He has set water and fire before you: stretch forth your hand to that which you will.

---

[57] *Counsel* is an intellective activity. This agrees with what we said about *volition* being made by means of a *reflection* which concludes, so to speak, with the assent of the will.

Before man is life and death, good and evil: that which he shall choose shall be given him.'[58]

Article 8.
Corollaries about freedom of the will

181. Several important corollaries follow from what we have said about the freedom of the human will.

1. The degree of freedom depends upon the intensity of the stimuli[59] and the consequent ease with which they become *reasons* for acting.

2. If human beings possessed only direct knowledge without the presence of other stimuli acting as reasons contrary to the norm of direct knowledge, the will would be free to the highest degree. Direct knowledge does not bind, but simply directs the will.

3. A good will, which adapts itself and assents with simplicity to direct knowledge, does not lessen its freedom by its assent and the enjoyment it procures for itself from the truth.

4. When the will starts to give way before imaginary and false reasons contrary to direct knowledge, it begins by that very fact to restrict and damage itself by losing its freedom. As long as these deceitful, utilitarian reasons, contrary to truth, continue to be present, the will can no longer adapt itself and assent to truth easily.

5. But even when faced with the false reasons which it has endowed with various degrees of conviction, the will retains the power to lessen the force it has given them provided it perseveres in its efforts to do so. And this requires time.

---

[58] Ecclesiasticus 15. 14–18 [*Douai*]
[59] This arises from the unity of the feeling and willing subject. The sensible stimulus acts on the feeling subject, which is also intellective and thus moves the will to satisfy the stimuli of the bodily sense.

6

THE POWERS INVOLVED IN MORAL ACTS

Article 1.
Moral powers in themselves and by participation

182. As we have seen, there are two kinds of moral powers: those moral in themselves and those moral by participation. The former direct the practical judgment, the latter regulate affections and external acts. External moral acts presuppose the power of acting externally, which becomes a moral power when it is moved by moral affectivity. Moral affectivity presupposes the power of affectivity, which becomes a moral power when moved by practical esteem. But the power of practical esteem or judgment does not become moral because it is itself the moral power. We must now see which powers are involved with the power regulating the practical judgment.

Article 2.
Moral intellect

183. The spirit is endowed with intellect in so far as it sees being. When being is used as moral law, the intellect is appropriately called moral intellect. *Moral intellect* is therefore the faculty of intellect dependent on the first moral law.

Article 3.
Moral reason

184. Reason is the faculty enabling us to apply being, to render perceptions intellective, to separate ideas from these perceptions, and to integrate and unite the ideas in judgments and reasonings. The power to apply being as moral law can be called moral reason. *Moral reason* is the power to form perceptions and ideas as moral laws, to deduce secondary laws from the first, universal law, and to define just and

unjust actions. In other words, it is the faculty for making moral judgments.

Article 4.
Eudaimonological reason

185. *Reason* is called *eudaimonological* when it is concerned with human happiness. It is the power to apply being as a rule for judging our own subjective good.

Article 5.
Practical reason

186. *Practical reason* is the capacity of voluntary reflection to form decisive esteem of an object, and consequently, of an action concerning it; an esteem followed immediately by decisive love, which itself is followed by the external act.[60]

The power of forming the decisive esteem or practical judgment, in which the affection is rooted, vacillates in its preference between moral and eudaimonological reasons. After considering them both, it makes the practical judgment or esteem, which activates the affection.

187. *Practical reason* acts as a kind of arbiter between the *utility* and the *probity* of actions. It judges what is better for us to do here and now, and is based on moral as well as eudaimonological reasons. Hence both ethical and eudaimonological reason are included in *practical reason*. Both are theoretical and speculative and reduced to practice by an appropriate function of the spirit. Properly speaking it is this function of the spirit that constitutes *practical reason*, and it produces its effect when a human being is about to act. He compares the moral and eudaimonological motives, weighs their importance, and finally pronounces his interior

---

[60] The faculties of intellect and reason are unique, but have different *functions*. For the sake of brevity and simplicity, these two general faculties are commonly divided according to their different functions into subordinate, special faculties. Thus instead of using the awkward phrase 'reason in so far as it makes judgments about moral things', we abbreviate it simply to 'moral reason'. [. . .]

operative judgment. Affection and action follow immediately. This final judgment, immediately preceding human action, is called 'practical' to distinguish it from 'speculative' judgment. 'Practical reason' is the faculty controlling it.

Article 6.
Moral reason is the source of every law except the first

188. The judgments made by moral reason are secondary laws contained in the first, supreme law as species in the genus. For example, I make a judgment of moral reason when I judge that an intelligent nature is worthy of such respect that I cannot consider it as a means to my own end without offending its dignity as a being having its own end. In making this judgment moral reason uses the idea of being as its rule to measure subsistent beings and determine the degree, mode and quantity of their being. It sees that intellective being is of such a mode and nature that it contains the excellence of 'end'. This excellence places the intellective being above all non-intellective beings, which are ordered to it as means, and not it to them.

189. If we consider the obligatory force manifested in this judgment of moral reason, the judgment becomes a decree or moral law. The truth of this is seen in the following formula: 'Intelligent being has in itself the nature of end, and therefore *must* be acknowledged as such.'

Article 7.
The definition of moral conscience

190. If I make a practical judgment based on eudaimonological, non-moral motives, I sin, and certain affections and immoral actions follow. When I sin, I am conscious of sinning, and experience an interior bitterness. What is this consciousness or conscience, and where does it come from?

I am conscious of sinning because I feel the force of the law, that is, of direct knowledge, which is law in me. Instead of assenting to it as I should, I violate it; I judge myself, declaring my practical judgment evil and immoral.

191. I call this judgment of self *moral conscience*, and I agree with popular opinion that it is not a *practical judgment*. It is in fact 'a speculative judgment on the morality of my practical judgment and its consequences.'

We say we must act according to our conscience. This can only mean that we must appreciate and judge things for what they are worth, love them proportionately, and then act according to this well ordered love. Conscience, therefore, is not a practical judgment; it is a speculative, moral judgment determining how the practical judgment must be made.

192. It not only accompanies but even precedes the practical judgment, indicating how it must be made. And when the practical judgment has been made, conscience approves or disapproves of it. This explains the traditional distinction between *antecedent, concomitant* and *consequent* conscience.

This clear definition of conscience could help, I believe, to remove much of the obscurity and uncertainty found in writings on ethics.

7

THE TWO ELEMENTS OF MORAL ACTS

Article 1.
Law and will as the two elements of moral acts

193. All we have said so far demonstrates that moral acts consist of two elements: 1. *law*, and 2. *will* in harmony with the law.

The moral law is the direct knowledge or ideas of things. But universal being is the first idea, the form of all other ideas. It is therefore the first law, and the form of all laws.

The will, harmonising with the law by an act of *voluntary reflection*,[61] acknowledges things exactly as they are in direct knowledge. This voluntary acknowledgement is a judgment and an esteem of things *proportionate* to their true value and free of arbitrary alteration; we find pleasure in what is good in things and willingly surrender ourselves to that good. In a word, we assent to truth without resistance or repugnance. From this honest esteem flows pleasure in truth which, in harmony with reason, provides us with a love of all things without exclusion according to their merit. With this love as a foundation, the human being acts, and acts justly if his love is rightly ordered.

194. If moral acts are composed of these two elements a treatise on ethics would have to study them carefully and deduce from this *twofold principle* the whole science of moral discipline. Consequently, I think it would be helpful to give a brief description of the deduction, but only a brief description as I am concerned simply with the foundations of ethics.

Article 2.
The imputability of acts

195. Moral acts are *imputed* to the praise or blame of their author. The degree of imputation varies according to the

---

[61] This reflection, which is always voluntary ('freely willed'), is also *positively willed*. This is another element for judging the moral perfection of the agent, as we shall explain shortly.

gravity of the law, and according to the efficacy of will present in the good or guilty act. The will's efficacy is measured according to the degree of *intensity* by which it is drawn to the act, as well as by the *degree* of *freedom* it enjoys.

Article 3.
The distinction between sin and fault

196. Every evil action therefore has a double relationship: to the *law* violated and to the *free will* violating the law. Hence the distinction made by St. Thomas between *sin* and *fault*: the notion of sin consists in the act of the will rejecting the law; the notion of fault lies in this freedom of the will. When the will necessarily but not freely turns from the law, its act is indeed immoral, and in this sense is a sin, because both conditions, law and will, are present. But the act cannot be imputed as culpable because the will of the person committing it is not free. St. Thomas writes: 'Just as the notion of *evil* is more extensive than that of *sin*, so the notion of sin is more extensive than that of *fault*. For an act is said to be culpable or praiseworthy when imputed to the person performing it. To praise or blame simply means to impute to someone the goodness or malice of his action. But the act is imputed to the agent when he is able to control it; this happens in every voluntary act[62] because a human being controls his actions through his will — therefore only voluntary (*free*) acts of good and evil are subject to praise or blame; and in them evil, sin and fault are the same thing.'[63]

---

[62] St. Thomas is speaking of a free will, as the context shows.
[63] *Sicut malum est in plus quam peccatum, ita peccatum est in plus quam culpa. Ex hoc enim dicitur actus culpabilis vel laudabilis, quod imputatur agenti: nihil enim est aliud laudari vel culpari, quam imputari alicui malitiam vel bonitatem sui actus. Tunc enim actus imputatur agenti, quando est in potestate ipsius, ita quod habeat dominium sui actus: hoc autem est in omnibus actibus voluntariis, quia per voluntatem homo dominium sui actus habet. Unde relinquitur, quod bonum vel malum in solis actibus voluntariis constituit rationem laudis vel culpae: in quibus idem est malum, peccatum, et culpa. S.T.* I-II, q. 21, art. 2.

Article 4.
Moral goodness is 'productive' and 'perfective'

197. We have seen that there are two kinds of good, substantial good and the good of perfection. When each of these is the work of a will, it is moral good, because good is moral when produced by the will. In the subject that wills, therefore, there is *goodness* that I shall call 'productive', and *goodness* that is 'perfective', which are very different in nature. When substantial good is produced, no real being pre-exists but only the possibility and idea of the being to be produced; when 'perfective' good is in question, a real being pre-exists which as term of the will and love receives the act of goodness.

198. A possible being, which is only an idea and nothing in itself, cannot make itself a term of the will; it is only the law, norm and measure by which subsistent being can be known, judged and measured. But the will is directed only to subsistent being, in which its practical judgment terminates as in its end. Hence we see that *possible being without a corresponding subsistent being* cannot induce moral obligation or give rise to a moral judgment. Two elements are always necessary for a judgment, possible being (the *means* for judging) and subsistent being (the *thing* judged). No obligation can arise, therefore, towards mere possibilities; no one can be required to produce them. This is *moral liberty*.

Clearly, then, the creator is not required by a moral necessity to give existence to creation, because creation cannot demand anything before it exists.

199. Furthermore, a human being is not required to generate other humans, because, not existing, they cannot be the object of any duty (duties towards fictitious creations of our own imagination are not in question, of course). The absence of substantial good, therefore, is neither good nor evil. It is a simple negation, not a privation, and negation presupposes neither productive action nor a moral author of productive action.

Article 5.
Gratitude

200. Although the production of the good of existence does not originate in any moral necessity, an intelligent creature is a good to itself from the first moment of its production. It must therefore be grateful to the one who was the cause willing the good of its existence.

201. We may wonder perhaps how *gratitude* arises and how it is connected with the principles I have enunciated. It is a feeling consisting of many emotions, and is difficult to analyse. But I hope I can explain sufficiently how these affections constitute the matter of moral duty.

I love myself; I am a good to myself — there is nothing moral here, only an instinct, a subjective good. Nevertheless I know I do not exist through myself but through the will of another who has given me existence. The love I have for myself and my existence is naturally directed towards the cause that produced me. I consider this cause good to me, as the origin of my good, and therefore I love it because everything considered good is loved. This natural feeling conforms to the truth, as it is true that I am a good to myself, and the cause producing me is good relative to me. Hence, because I have a concept of what caused me, I must judge and value what caused me for what it effectively is.

202. Hence the creator or generator does not, by his act, become better in himself. No moral law approves or disapproves his act, because the law comes from the subsistent being we perceive, which does not yet exist. Thus, one of the two elements necessary for moral acts is missing, and the act is nothing more than an entirely free production of the will. However, once the intelligent being is created or generated, what caused it acquires a new goodness relative to the intelligent being. This new relationship makes no change in the moral state of the cause but produces a duty in the being who has received existence.

203. A further observation can be made about the affections contained in the feeling of gratitude which originates from the knowledge of a good received. No moral dignity is acquired by the person who receives good, because the

increase of good is only subjective. However, if the good is one of perfection, the moral dignity lies entirely with the giver for whom the good is objective. For the receiver the good is subjective.

204. Human beings are compelled by conscience to seek moral good. Unless they are depraved, the voice of reason disinterestedly and generously indicates to them two noble sentiments when they receive good.

205. First, a feeling of esteem and love for the moral dignity of their benefactor. This sentiment must, by its nature, be happy and joyful if unopposed by an evil will. Second, a feeling of confusion, as they consider that they have *received* rather than *given*. Such a feeling, if unopposed by the will, shows itself in *self-abasement*, tempered with gentle unease. This self-abasement merits praise and approval in the measure that the will abandons itself to it, because self-abasement conforms to their true state, even if contrary to unworthy self-love. These upright sentiments, which accord with reason and arise spontaneously from the ideas of *benefactor* and *benefited* (direct knowledge), can be furthered by the action of the will. If they are, the human being exercises the virtue of gratitude in its fulness. If the will opposes them, the human being sins in various ways against this most fitting obligation.

Article 6.
Moral goodness as 'perfective'

207. The will is good when it acknowledges and enjoys things as presented in the ideas extracted from the perceptions of the things, but evil when the opposite is true. In the first case, delight and love begin in the one who wills; in the second, the will opposes things, experiences sadness, and hatred enters in.

208. The act of honestly acknowledging and enjoying the worth of things (and more particularly, of persons) can be carried out with greater or lesser efficacy. We may ask, at what point does *duty* or moral obligation begin? And where does *counsel* start, which is a higher good than obligation? Can the will love intelligent beings excessively?

Being is infinitely lovable, and when the will inclines to *being as such*, acknowledging its infinite worth, no limit can be placed on the will's efficacy. The consequent indefinite increase of its levels of efficacy and love is simply an *indefinite perfecting* of the moral agent, who can always increase his moral excellence without ever attaining the infinitely distant summit. But if there can be no excess in the levels of efficacy, the immorality of the will is in the *disorder* with which it loves being itself.

209. Order is intrinsic to being, as we have said, and being must be loved according to this order. To love disordinately is to hate being. This is so true that if, for example, I were to love *things* more than *persons*, I would hate being. My esteem would remove from persons the element of being which raises them far above things; by not acknowledging this element, I have annihilated it from my reflective, willing thought, and hatefully destroyed it with my will. If I were to give things an element of being which places them above persons, I would not love being but only a fiction and an illusion, nothingness. And to love nothingness or false being is hatred of real being. To violate, by our esteem and love, the order of being is intrinsically repugnant and contrary to truth and virtue. Our duty and obligation is to appreciate and love in perfect proportion to this order.

210. We can now determine the dividing line between what is obligatory and what is morally good but not obligatory. Obligation extends to the distribution of our appreciation and love in proportion to the order of being, without any change to the order. It does not extend further. It does not include the level of esteem and love we give to beings, provided their proportion and order have been safeguarded. The level of esteem and love depends on our judgment. In its turn, the degree of our moral goodness corresponds to the degree of our esteem and well ordered love.

211. A vast area, therefore, is open for free, spontaneous moral goodness and perfection. All human beings can perform their duties perfectly, by maintaining right order in their judgments, affections and actions. But some people will be infinitely more perfect and excellent than others because stronger in will and more intense in action. Because this

action unites them more closely to being, they can rejoice and take real pleasure in it, loving it all the more.

Article 7.
Duties with a corresponding right in those towards whom the duties are exercised

212. We must love human beings according to order. Although this love includes our moral duties towards our neighbour, it does not necessarily mean that our neighbour has a strict right to our love, claiming it as their *own*. We are the masters of our love, accountable only to the law and to the supreme legislator in whom the law resides. People can rightly object to our hatred for them, because they are the objects of injustice, but hatred does not take from them what in fact is truly theirs. My love is not their *property*, nor do I belong to them. It is the force of law that imposes the duty on me.

213. The word *right*, as I understand it here, refers to each one's *property*, that which is *mine* by right. Hence, if I damage another's right, I harm him; I injure the person and violate his right.

Duties towards my neighbour, therefore, in whom there is a corresponding right, are contained in the formula: 'Do not harm your fellow human being.' Human beings have only one right: not to be harmed, not to be despoiled of what belongs to them. They have no other rights, in the sense defined.

Having a right implies, as a consequence, that we can protect and defend ourselves with force against anyone who would harm us or take what is ours. On the other hand, as long as hatred is concealed in the heart, we have no way of defending ourselves against it. Hence, love and hatred are not a matter of right.

214. The rights of human beings therefore correspond to negative, prohibitive duties. But there are also positive duties, such as love of our neighbour, who can never be the property of another. Thus duties have their origin in law, not in human rights. Some duties then forbid us to harm our neighbour,

while the law itself permits our neighbour to redress any harm done to him, and gives him a right to do so.

Duties towards human beings in whom there are corresponding rights are called duties of *justice*,[64] other duties are duties of *charity*.

Article 8.
Duties towards oneself

215. Ethics has for its sole aim the good of intelligent beings; hence God and humans are its objects.[65] The *subject as such* is naturally excluded, as we have seen. An act is not moral because it concerns and pleases *me* but because it conforms to the truth (direct knowledge) which is essentially impersonal, having its own efficacy without dependence on any human person. Are duties to oneself, therefore, excluded?

216. 'Duties' to oneself produced directly by emanations from the feeling which is 'myself', are excluded. But because I am a human, intelligent being, an *object* of contemplation of my own mind, whatever is due to human nature is due to me. Duties to myself are the same as duties to all other human beings (and modern sensist philosophy has done much harm in the world by making a separate category of these duties to oneself and declaring them to be the unique, supreme, universal class).

217. There is then no basic, essential difference between duties to oneself and to one's fellow human beings. However, duties to oneself do contain something particular. Ethics tells me I must desire the good of human nature, whether the nature is in me or elsewhere. This is a law common to all, without exception or special privilege, and applies to myself as much as to all humans beings. But how do I know what is good for human nature? How do I know what human nature needs to help and please it, or what harms and displeases it?

[64] The word 'justice' is used in a strict sense: this justice is the foundation of civil law.

[65] Acknowledgement of God by voluntary reflection is the principle of adoration and of all acts of religion; it is the highest motive for love by human beings.

218. I cannot know from others, but know only from myself, by the feeling I have of 'myself'. All the different sensations (pleasure, pain, needs, instincts, etc.) that modify 'myself' are experiences indicating to me what takes place in my fellow human beings: what is good or evil for human nature, what it desires, rejects or avoids, what it seeks as its perfection. It is from my own fundamental, substantial feeling[66] that I acquire the idea of 'human being' (direct knowledge), and this idea becomes the rule by which I know what good I must desire for such a being. Only feeling *perceives* subsistences, and from its perceptions ideas are extracted. The *subject*, 'myself', a *feeling*, gives me an experience which becomes the rule for my treatment of all other human beings. This explains why the subject, 'myself', is found in the divine precepts, and why there are two precepts, not three: 'You will love the Lord your God with your whole heart, your whole soul, and all your mind; this is the first and greatest commandment. The second is like to this: you will love your neighbour AS YOURSELF.' And in case anyone should think there might be other commandments, the divine lawgiver immediately added: 'On these two commandments depend the whole law and the prophets.'[67]

Yourself does not constitute a third precept; it is found in the precepts as the example of our duty to love human beings. *Yourself* expresses a subject from which comes not the moral law but knowledge of human beings and their needs. We would know nothing about human nature and others' needs if we did not have the perception of ourselves and the experience of what happens in us.

219. I have said that the law, commanding us to respect human nature as end, has no essential, intrinsic difference whether applied to ourselves or to others. Nevertheless, there is an accidental difference in the way it is carried out although this difference is not an exception or a law of special privilege arrogated by the subject. As regards myself, I can have a greater or lesser *opportunity* to put the law into practice; I can in varying degrees be helped by feeling or instinct in the faith-

---

[66] Teaching on the fundamental feeling is presented in *The Origin of Thought* [695 ss].
[67] Mt 22. 37-40

ful execution of what the law imposes on me; I can have the opportunity to carry it out more fully and extensively. This is true of the law regarding human nature when applied to myself only and not to my fellow human beings.

220. As far as the law applies to me, I have an inclination, a great interest and need to carry out the law or at least not to violate it. This may remove my liberty, which is an element of merit, and reduce or cancel the merit in carrying out the duty, but the duty still remains, commanding me. If I violate it, I am guilty in the measure that the violation was *easy* or difficult to avoid. In addition, I am always in my own company but not always with others, and can therefore more *frequently* and actually respect human nature in myself rather than in them. Finally, because I know all the needs of my nature, I can practise the law more *extensively* towards myself.

These three facts give duty towards myself a specific form: nature clearly entrusts me with the special responsibility of helping myself. It is a specific form of duty intended by nature and the creator, and I perform it in respectful obedience to the dispositions of the Being who has made all things. For this reason an accidental difference between the law of respect for human nature as applied to myself and as applied to others comes from a superior law, and not from some odious privilege in my favour. In the gospel precepts of charity, which are an enunciation of the natural law, this higher law is expressed by the word NEIGHBOUR, precisely because no one is more a neighbour to myself than myself! The word NEIGHBOUR dictates the execution of the universal law in conformity with the intentions of nature and God.

221. A further observation may help to illustrate more clearly this wonderful gospel word, NEIGHBOUR. The needs of nature are either common or particular. Common needs are those always present to the human being; particular needs result from some accidental relationship. For example, the need for food is common and constant, but the need to love children arises from the particular relationship between father and children. The moral law requires us to desire all possible good for human beings, and, if we are able, to fulfil all the needs of nature. Nature itself requires this, and these require-

ments of nature are precisely moral obligation. Consequently, a father is obliged to co-operate with the love nature has given him for his children. And the care of these children is a duty exercised by the father to himself, although it would be more accurate to say, exercised towards human nature present in himself through the relationship of fatherhood.

222. The subjective *instinct*, therefore, that moves the father to love and rear his children is not the same as *duty*. In human beings it becomes a duty because of the reasonableness of the instinct, but where reason is lacking, as in animals, it would be a pure instinct. The *reasonableness* of the instinct means the need reason has to acknowledge human nature, which we mentally conceive, for what it is, and as such, meriting love — if we respect human nature, we desire for it all possible good. Hence, human nature's desire to love the child, as expressed in fatherhood, is good, and nature must be helped and supported in this good. The father must love his children, not because they are his (a subjective principle) or a privilege granted to him, but because he is a father and they are children (a general principle and a law common to all); his love is not a good particular to him alone but a good for all human nature, which he must respect and love in himself. Anything that does not originate from this great principle, or adds to it or subtracts from it, is not duty but natural instinct, and has nothing to do with morality.

223. A father then sees human beings in his children and as human beings owes them what he owes every human being. But in addition to human nature, he has the quality of father, by which he owes to himself the love, care and education of his children. But also as father he must show reverence for human nature, because it is in him precisely as father.

The duty of loving and caring for children is confirmed and sanctioned by a superior duty. This duty requires the father to obey divine Providence in the performance of the responsibility he has received from Providence.

224. The rights of children in respect of parents therefore are only those of human beings, but parents *owe* to themselves and to God the care of their children, not only as *human beings* but also as *children*. Here, we could say,

subjective instinct contributes to law; we also understand the nature of duties towards ourselves and the force of the word NEIGHBOUR sanctified in the Gospel.

225. After all, why does a father owe himself the love and care of his children? This duty springs from the natural connection between him and his children — the nature of father binds him to them. He is, in fact, their NEIGHBOUR. This word includes every natural relationship of human beings, and therefore every particular duty.

But, if we consider the matter further, we may ask whether, amongst the relationships, there is any that is closer than the one we have with ourselves, and the answer is definitely 'no'. Indeed there cannot be a more absolute closeness, if we are allowed to use such an expression of the relationship of identity. Hence, it was fitting to take this *maximum* closeness as absolute norm and rule, as the Gospel did when it says: 'You will love YOUR NEIGHBOUR AS YOURSELF.'

We conclude then as follows. The law is universal: 'human nature must be respected and its good desired.'

226. The *good* of human nature is indicated by natural human instincts and inclinations, directed by the law towards certain persons rather than others, according to the persons' circumstances. This loving preference for certain people is called 'NEIGHBOURSHIP' by the gospel; it originates in the inclination we have to ourselves. 'Neighbourship' means simply closeness, the natural connection with ourselves. 'Ourself' therefore is the starting point of 'neighbourship' and distance

227. Consequently, every natural bond binding human beings is preserved and prescribed, because to desire the good of human nature is to desire what human nature desires. This natural desire and love constitute the bond of 'neighbourship', as the Gospel shows by its use of the word NEIGHBOUR in the parable of the good Samaritan. In the parable our neighbour is the one who loves more and, relative to the one loved, gives greater help and assistance. The statement of the law as YOU SHALL LOVE YOUR NEIGHBOUR AS YOURSELF is perfect and divine, and contains within itself the duties to ourselves, expressed in the place most fitting for them.

Index of Persons

Numbers in italics refer to paragraphs and footnotes in the Preface; numbers in romans refer to paragraphs and footnotes in the text.

Alexander of Hales fn. 11
Ambrose fn. 15
Aristotle *10*; fn. 11
Augustine 61, fn. 36

Bentham 86
Bonaventure 11
Bossuet 17

Cicero 10, 81

Epicurus *10*

Gioia *10*, 86

Helvetius 86

Ivo of Chartres 12

Jerome 11

Kant *2*, 15, 16, 46

Locke 18

Plato fns. 17, 27, *title page*

Romagnosi 86

Thomas Aquinas 42, 54, 196; fns. 41, 62

Zanotti, Francesco Maria *10*

General Index

Numbers in italics refer to paragraphs and footnotes in the Preface; numbers in romans refer to paragraphs and footnotes in the body of the work.

Acknowledgement
 begins the moral act 141
 by the will, of a thing's worth 143, 148
 esteem and 172
 of the truth as supreme duty 169
 refusal of 173, 174
 supreme principle of morality 167

Affections
 actions and 127 ss, 159
 follow esteem 159
 freedom and 133 ss
 nature of 135

Art (*in sense of* skill *or* activity)
 good and 5, 6
 theory and 4, 7

Ascetics
 definition 9

Autonomy
 Kant's 15

Being
 absolute 61, 82, 103-105, 107
 as activity 5
 as first moral law 4, 8, 11
 as light 7, 9, 11, 12, 94
 as truth 7, 168
 degrees of, measured by intelligence 96, 97
 dignity of intelligent subject and 66
 evil and 43, 44, 176
 form of intelligence 4
 good and 41, 42, 58, 69
 hatred of 209
 inanimate things and fn. 29
 intelligence and absolute 61, 113
 loved by human beings 94, 113, 208
 loved in its order 105, 111
 moral judgments and 4, 6, 11
 negation and privation of 44
 objective 82
 order of 38, 92-94
 seen by the human mind 82
 substantial and accidental 52
 the will relative to possible and subsistent 198

Bliss, *see* **Happiness**

Christianity
 moral law and 9, 11, 12

Concept
 of good 33, 42, 50, 60
 retained in a synthetic state 34

Conscience
 speculative judgment 191
 three kinds of 192

Counsel
 intellective activity fn. 57
 obligation and 208

Desire
 knowledge and 25
 of lesser good 99
 relative to good 22, 27, 49

Dignity
 human 104
 of intelligent subject 66-67

Doubts
 cause of 165

Duties
 division of applied ethics *14*
 of father towards children 221-225
 superior 223
 towards neighbour 212-214
 towards oneself 216-220

Economics
 definition 9

Enjoyment
 good and 24

knowledge and 75, 81
of perfections 29

Error
effect of voluntary reflection 153, 158
impossibility of 11
persuasion about 164
pride taken in 160

Essence
as rule of a being's good 36
complete and abstract 38, 40

Esteem
affection and 159
as an acknowledgement 172
decisive 186
dependent on a judgment 161
element of love 136
practical 137-138
reasonable and unreasonable 160
speculative 138

Ethics
applied *11*, 13
as an art *fn. 4*
definition *11*
division of *14*
duty and 85
eudaimonology and *10*, 86
human art and *4-6*
moral habits and *fn. 6*
morality and *11, fn. 3*
object of *9*, 215
principle of 70
pure *11, 12*
supreme importance of 7
two sections of *fn. 5*
twofold elements of moral acts and 194

Eudaimonology
definition *9*, 46
differs from ethics 46, 62, 86
ethics and *10*
subjective good and 51, 69
see also **Happiness**

Evil
anything harmful to a being 36, 39, 56
being and 43, 44
moral 99
negation and privation as 44
of destruction and of deterioration 55-57

Feeling (sense)
existence and 26, 32, fn. 17
fundamental 218
good and 74, 77, 79
human subject and 79
order and 36
passive power 115
perceives subjectively 115
perfections and 25-29, 31
relative to ideas 32, 218

Freedom
affections and 132-134
exercise of 139
of the will 132-143, 153, 177

God
absolute good 61
as actuation of mental being 107
free to create 198
perception of 67
reasoning and fn. 34
relative to vision of universal, potential being 67, 82, 103-105, 113
source of all good 64
source of human dignity 105

Good
absolute 58, 60, 61, 63, 64, 82, fn. 40
absolute notion of 58, 60, 73
animals and 49
as object of faith fn. 34
being and 41, 54, 69
bodily feeling and 74
collision with other 99
concept of 33, 50, 60
definition 21
desire and 22, 23, 25, 27
difference between idea of good and fn. 32
double 53
enjoyment and 24, fn. 35
finality of 54
human beings and 62-65, 92
instinct and 87
intelligence measuring degrees of 96
kinds of 31
non-sensitive beings and 30, 31, 49, fn. 29
notion of degrees of 60
objective 73, 76-84, 89
of existence and of perfection 52-54
perfections and 23-40
relative 49, 50, 58

relative notion of 58, 60, 73
sensations and 39
spiritual and corporeal 64, 65
subjective 48, 49, 76-81, fn. 39
substantial 197-199
will and 63, 101
see also **Concept, Moral Good**

Gratitude
for existence 200
moral dignity of giver and receiver 203
origin of 201, 202
two sentiments for good received 204, 205
will and 205, 206

Guilt, *see* **Sin**

Happiness
a subjective good 47, 51
bliss as final good 63, 67
for human beings 62-65, 67, 68
virtue and *10*
see also **Eudaimonology**

Hatred
depravity of will and 98
irrational 145-147
love of lesser good 99
result of seeing things as bad 135

Heteronomy
Kant's 16

Human being
free of obligation to generate 199
'myself' as rule for treating —s 218, 225, 226
two active faculties of 116, fn. 40
two passive faculties of 115, fn. 40

Human Nature
common and particular needs of 221
finality in 105
'myself' as source of knowledge of 218
respect for and good of 225-227
weakness and nobility of 103

Idea of (universal) being
absolute being and 103, 104
Alexander of Hales and fn. 11
as notion measuring degrees of being 97

differs from being fn. 32
dignity of intelligent subject and 66
divine characteristics of 15
first and innate idea 12
'form' of intelligence 4
infinite capacity of 103
judgments and 4, 69
measure of good in all natures 45, 84
moral law and 8, 11, 12, 17
possible or initial fn. 32
principle of eudaimonology 47
vision of God and 67
see also **Being**

Ideas
as reasons and notions fn. 1
as truth 168
coldness of 142, 143, fn. 48
difference between having and using fn. 2
reflection on first 142

Immorality
essence and principle of 176
failure to acknowledge worth of something 168
love of lesser good 99
violation of principle of contradiction 176

Imputability
nature of 195

Instinct
active power 116, fns. 40, 44
cause of reflection 125
duty arising from 222
good and 83, 87
inclines to pleasure and happiness fns. 40 43
or stimulus as source of morality fn. 28
two —s fn. 43
will mingled with fn. 49

Intellect, Intelligence
a law of 34
as a feeling fn. 33
beings viewed as ends by 101
conceives objectively 115
counsel is activity of fn. 57
degrees of being and 96
double aspect of thoughts fn. 33
good and 49, 63, 65, 80-81, 83, 84, 87

measuring degrees of moral goodness 98, 99
moral 183
opposition between possible things and fn. 19
order and 91, 92, 95
passive power 115
perceiving objectively 13, 14
perception of God and 67
sense and 82

Intellective Sense (Intellective Feeling)
absolute being and 67, 82
good enjoyed by 75, 81
known to early thinkers fn. 36
nature of fn. 33

Intelligent Beings
as 'ends' 101-102, 113

Judgments
being and 6, 69, 97, 98
different effects of reflective 155-157
moral reason and 188, 189
practical 137 ss, 179, 180, 182, 186, 187
true 168
two elements of 198
see also **Moral Judgments**

Justice
as foundation of civil law 214 fn.
duties of 214
essentially present in knowledge 81
esteem and 161
found only in act of reason 84
harmony and 166
honoured by all peoples 106
idea of 94
obligation of *8*

Knowledge
acts of 13, 74, 80
desire and 25
direct 118-120, 140-141, 153, 154, 164, 168, 193
enjoyment and 75
infinity of 66, 97
of good 26, 45, 66, 74, 89
reflection and 121-126, 140-156, 172
sensation and direct 142
truth of 161, 176
two acts of 163
unchangeable 176

Light of Reason, *see* **Reason**

Love
acts dependent on 128
esteem and 136-139
in intelligent beings 101, 105, 136
irrational 146, 147
nature of 128-137
of being 94, 99, 105, 208
of good 87, 99
of neighbour 218, 220, 221
practical 129, 132, 138

Mind
human actions and *11*
judgments and *3*, 3
sees being 82

Moral Actions
dignity of aim and term of 109
dignity of author of 109
eight steps of 150, 151
moral law and 1, 2, 6
nature of 162
tend towards being in its order 100
two elements of 193, 194

Moral Anthropology
division of pure ethics *14*

Moral Formulas
ethics and *11, 14*

Moral Good
as objective good 83, 84, 87
different degrees possible 211
good and 72
order in 100
perfective and productive 197
truth and 169
twofold dignity of 106-109
voluntary reflection, starting point of 148
will and 89, 90, 114

Moral Judgments
being and 6, 69
first law and 4, 6
practical 137

Moral Law
actions and 1, 2, 6
as a notion 1, 2, fn. 1

as direct knowledge 193
difference between existence and promulgation of fn. 2
division of applied ethics *14*
final and first *3*, *8*, *17*, 193
formula of 7, 85, 88, 94, 110-113
human spirit and 18
in tradition 9-12
in union of subject and object 19
'myself' and 219, 220
promulgation of 2, fn. 2
reason and 184
universal *11*

Moral Logic
division of pure ethics *14*

Moral Powers
two kinds of 182

Moral Sciences, *see* **Ethics**

Morality
a definition of 114
dependent on subject and object 17
dignity of 107, 108
idea of being and 8, 87
instinct or stimulus and fn. 28
of actions 1, 2, 6
principle of 8

Neighbourship
bond of 227
'ourself' as starting point of 226

Nominalism
origin of fn. 21

Nomology
division of pure ethics *14*

Notion
as law 1, 2
human beings born with fn. 13
interdependence of —s 3
of good and real good 60
the ultimate 3

Object
attributing human characteristics to 16, 18
confused with subject 14, 15, 86
in intellective perception 13

moral law and 19
order in 95

Obligation
acknowledgement of knowledge and 173-176
extension of 210
force of 171, 178, 179
possibilities and 198

Order
abstract essence as principle of 40
as perfection 35, 36
being and 38, 41, 93-95, fn. 24
complete essence as the end of 40
direct knowledge and 176
light of reason and 88
the understanding and 36, 92, 95, fn. 23
to be loved by the will 101

Pedagogics
definition *9*

Perception
intellective 13, 14

Perfection
as order 36
division of sciences of *9*
eudaimonology and *9*
feeling and fn. 22
good and *8*
of human beings *8*, *9*
see also **Good**

Perfections
common sense and 30
feeling (sense) and 25-29, 31, 32
nature of 27, 30
origin of ideas of 34

Personality
intelligent beings as 'end' and 101
located in the will fn. 44

Persuasion
about truth and error 164
as a judgment 161
reasonable and unreasonable 160

Philosophy
division of *1*, *2*
practical and theoretical *1*, *fn. 1*

Politicians
different judgments made by 156, 157

Politics
definition *10*

Reason
definition of 7
eudaimonological 185
fallibility of 7
light of 7, 12, 87, 88, fn. 14
moral 184, 188, 189
moral law and 7, 94, 178
practical 186, 187
theoretical and practical *fn. 2*
will and sufficient 177, 180

Reasoning
definition of 7
God and fn. 34

Reflection
as starting point of moral goodness 148
cause of 125
freedom and 139, 141
knowledge and 123, 141, 142, 171
object of intellectual act and 95
positively willed fn. 61
power of voluntary 147
three types of acts of 124

Relationship
between absolute and objective good 82
between cause and effect 32
between corporeal and spiritual substances of human being 62, 64, 65
between feeling and perfection fn. 22
between intellect and order 36
between persuasion, judgment and esteem 161
between subjective and objective good 76-81
between subsistences and possibilities 32
—s as division of applied ethics *14*

Remorse
origin of 171
reveals force of obligation 171

Right
regarding neighbour's love 213, 214

Scripture
human freedom in 180
light of reason and St. Paul fn. 14
love of neighbour and 218, 220-221, 224-227
moral goodness and truth synonymous in 169
upright person according to 170
source of goodness or evil and 148
source of people's endless doubts and 165

Sensations
direct knowledge and 142
morality and 17
phenomenon of fn. 18

Sense
perceives subsistent things 82
self-love and 83
see also **Intellective Sense**

Sensists
error of fn. 35

Sin
a lying to oneself 169
guilt and 196
practical judgment and 190

Statistics
different interpretations of 157

Subject
accidental perfections of 52
confused with object 14, 15, 86
divinisation of 15, 18
good and 48, 49, 75
moral law and 19
moral principle and *fn. 5*
moved by sensible stimuli fn. 59
passive to phenomena 90
self-love of 83
substance or specific essence of 52
tendency to perfection 53, 54
understanding and 80, 81

Telethics
definition *9*

Truth
    accepted or rejected by the will 145, 146
    acknowledgement of 169
    being as 7, 168
    ideas as 168
    knowledge and 163, 176
    moral goodness and, in scripture 169
    principle of morality 169
    type or norm of the mind 168
    upright person and 170

Virtue
    definition 90, 117
    human art and 7
    knowledge and 118-121
    reflection and 140-156

Vital Apprehension
    by will 148, 150

Vital Pleasure or Displeasure
    accompanying vital apprehension 149

Will
    absolute being and 105, 113
    active power 116, 117, fn. 40
    aim of acts of 101
    as principle of morality fn. 40
    being and 110, 111
    belief and 154
    definition of 118, 177
    definition of act of 126
    element of moral acts 193
    free 132-143, 153, 177
    gratitude and 206
    good and 63, 101
    good and bad 145, 146, 207
    instinct mingled with fn. 49
    judging morality of 98
    knowledge and 119-121, fn. 49
    love of persons and 112, 208
    moral faculty 110
    moral good and 89, 90, 92
    nature of 90, 115-117
    reflection and 122-126, 147, 148, 153, fn. 61
    personality and 90, 101, fn. 44
    process of action of 144-147
    sufficient reason and 177-180
    term or object of 198, fn. 41
    two standards of evil will 158
    vital apprehension by 148, 150